BE STILL AND KNOW . . .

SATURDAY M....... ....M
THE DAILY TELEGRAPH

BY

DENIS DUNCAN

Other books by Denis Duncan

A Day at a Time
a thought and a prayer for each day of a year

Creative Silence
with twenty meditation outlines

Health and Healing: A Ministry to Wholeness
an exposition of the healing ministry

Love, the Word that heals
reflections on St Paul's Hymn of Love
(I Corinthians, Chapter 13)

Here is my hand
the life and work of Alida Bosshardt, the
Salvation Army officer who served for 27 years
in the Red Light district of Amsterdam

*These titles are published by Arthur James Limited.
The latter two are out of print.*

Books edited by Denis Duncan

Through the Year with William Barclay
a Barclay thought for each day of a year

Every Day with William Barclay
further Barclay thoughts for each day of a year

Marching Orders
six months' Barclay thoughts for younger people

Marching On
a further six months' thoughts for younger people

Through the Year with J B Phillips
a Phillips thought for each day of a year

Through the Year with Cardinal Heenan
a Heenan thought for each day of a year

*These titles (excepting Through the Year with Cardinal
Heenan which is out of print) are now published by
Arthur James Limited*

BE STILL AND KNOW . . .

SATURDAY MEDITATIONS

FROM

THE DAILY TELEGRAPH

BY

DENIS DUNCAN

WITH A FOREWORD BY

CLIFFORD LONGLEY

Arthur James

BOOK PUBLISHERS

Arthur James Limited
4, Broadway Road,
Evesham, Worcs, WR11 6BH

telephone and fax: 01386 446 566

First published in 1994
Re-printed, September 1994
Re-printed, April 1995

British Library Cataloguing in Publication Data
Duncan, Denis
  Be Still and Know...: One Hundred
  Saturday Meditations from *The Daily Telegraph*
  I. Title
  242.2
        ISBN 0 85305 332 4

Cover design by
The Creative House, Saffron Walden, CB10 1EJ

Typeset by
Stumptype, London N20 0QG

Printed and bound by
The Guernsey Press Co. Ltd., Guernsey, Channel Islands

Dedication

I dedicate this book of Meditations to my wife, Ettie, who died on October 16th, 1993, and was for 51 years my partner on the way.

As she also served on the staff of *The Daily Telegraph* for over twenty years, particularly as secretary to Max Hastings, the Editor-in-Chief, it is the more appropriate that this volume of Saturday Meditations from that paper should be associated with her.

Contents

Part II — The Mystery of Suffering

Part III — People Matter

Part IV — Times and Seasons

Part V — The Healing Ministry

Foreword

We live in a culture which has reduced the spiritual to the psychological. That could even be the definition of the secular. At the same time, not many people would care to put their whole trust in psychology, as their ancestors placed their trust in God. As a result, we have become an orphan people, with nowhere to turn when we must turn somewhere.

Yet help is available under our very noses. It is not necessary to journey to the ashrams of India, or delve into the exotic mysteries of Zen or Yoga, in order to discover our spiritual roots. The Christian tradition lays all its riches before us, if we could only recognise them for what they are. But often we need a guide; and those with the necessary skills are few.

One guide with these gifts in abundance is Denis Duncan. This book gathers together in one place many of his articles which have been published in *The Daily Telegraph* under the heading "Meditations". For some of his readers this will be a reunion with old friends. Dr Duncan is a writer whose columns are cut out and kept, often to grow dog-eared within the folds of a wallet or purse. Such readers will find, to their pleasure, that in this case the total is even greater than the sum of its parts.

For other readers this will be a first introduction. It will be a rewarding encounter, not only for Christians but for those of any religion or none. Good spiritual writing transcends denominations, and can readily cross the boundaries between faiths. The ability to speak to people of all sorts and conditions is a sure test of true spirituality. That mysterious thing we exchange when we love and are loved, here on earth, is not a different thing from the love of God, of which the spiritual writer writes. To better understand the one is to better understand the other. And they are the entrance to the understanding of suffering, when love turns to pain.

What denies us access to the ancient and modern wisdom of Christianity is our own ignorance or fear, or that overfamiliarity which breeds contempt or indifference — or maybe, most of all, the hidden but pernicious influence of cultural fashion. Embarrassment at being thought 'religious' may be a poor reason for turning away from the only thing that is likely to help us, but in the present age it is a common reason nevertheless.

In the sensitive hands of Denis Duncan, the Christian faith becomes much more than a collection of texts or doctrines, and the Christian life something much deeper than a habit of church-going. It becomes an exploration and spiritual journey. "Through prayer, meditation and contemplation our level of spiritual awareness can change too . . ." he writes at one point. And later he explains "It is open to all who humbly seek and reverently ask, to be allowed . . . to touch and handle things unseen". There is a sense of beckoning on, a leading forth, in his writing which puts me in mind of some of the metaphysical poetry of George Herbert. Above all, neither of them make religion 'difficult' in a technical or intellectual way. Denis Duncan addresses people in their ordinary conditions and takes them as they are. I believe he also moves them on. It is a rare and extraordinary gift.

Clifford Longley
May 1994

Introduction

It has been my privilege and pleasure to contribute Saturday Meditations to *The Daily Telegraph* regularly since 1990. These have normally appeared in 13-week series, twice a year with another contributor writing the intervening series. This book of Meditations comprises seven such series, plus another three items also published in the *Telegraph*.

It is a matter for gratitude that a paper of national and international standing with a circulation of well over one million copies daily continues to include a religious meditation in its Saturday edition. That edition reaches an even wider circulation than on weekdays. I do not suggest for one moment that the Meditation is of interest to, or read by, all those millions of readers of the paper, but the volume of correspondence I receive indicates something of the value placed on the contributions. Letters come from members of all the denominations, from both clergy and lay, from people on the fringe of the faith, from Jewish readers and, at times, from those who are not religious at all.

Writing is an important medium of communication for me and represents an essential part of my commitment to "proclamation through preaching, print and publishing". I therefore value the opportunity this ministry provides.

Writing 500 words is however much more difficult than producing 2,000! The restriction is nevertheless a valuable exercise in discipline. Every word must count. Deviations and digressions cannot be entertained. The necessarily limited space allocated to the Meditation must be respected as must that demanding feature (long-familiar to me as Editor of *British Weekly*, the national religious newspaper, for thirteen years) — deadlines! But these pressures combine to compel the completion of the Meditation on time and to enforce the necessary "tightness" in writing so necessary in journalism.

The awareness I have of the scope and variety of the readership of *The Daily Telegraph* also influences my approach.

The Meditations will be read by clergy looking for some profundity of concept, academics used to an intellectual approach, lay people seeking inspiration and, possibly most of all, all kinds of individual people who long for pastoral support with spiritual insight. It is important to have empathy with *their* situation. That may well be one of profound suffering and inner pain. The Meditation must speak of the things that are "eternal", but also convince the reader that I am aware of the harsh, "temporal" realities with which people have to cope.

The pastoral purpose of the Meditations is evidenced by the number given to suffering, sharing and caring, and to love as the greatest of all Christian themes. The title of this volume of the Meditations is intended to underline the importance of stillness and silence in the spiritual life.

The Meditations are written week by week, taking account of the seasons of the Christian Year. As it happens my series have included Lent, Easter, Remembrance, Christmas and New Year. These have been collected together as the fourth section under the heading "Times and Seasons". I have gathered the remainder together under the headings "Spiritual Resources", "The Mystery of Suffering" and "People Matter" as, on re-reading the Meditations, these seemed to be the themes I have particularly emphasised.

Writing these as I do, not in long-planned series but simply responding to week-by-week needs, events and situations, there is inevitably repetition of references and phrases. To these, where it is desirable, I have drawn attention. I feel however that the Meditations should appear just as they did over the years. There are therefore references to, for example, the Gulf War, wars in Europe, even the Queen's "annus horribilis"! But they were written at that time and can, I feel, remain. Occasionally headings have been slightly adjusted as, over the years, one or two were too similar.

When my greatly beloved and honoured predecessor in this ministry, the late Bishop George Appleton, was asked by the then Editor of *The Daily Telegraph*, William Deedes (now Lord Deedes) to undertake this task, he was told that his function was to expound "the eternal verities", that is the great religious truths and realities. I have made that my guideline too, and so my Meditations aim to be just that, a reflecting on the great spiritual foundations of the faith. I hope I have succeeded in doing this with profound simplicity — that is, writing of deep things in understandable language. If through these Meditations, someone has been encouraged, inspired, comforted or sustained, then their purpose is met.

In quoting from the Psalms, I have used the numbering in the Authorised Version of the Bible. I have made frequent use too of William Barclay's translation of the New Testament which my own publishing house, Arthur James Limited, publishes in both hardback and paperback.

I am most grateful to Max Hastings, the Editor-in-Chief of *The Daily Telegraph* for his retaining and supporting the Meditation feature; to Christopher Hudson, the Features Editor in whose department lies responsibility for asking me to do these Meditations; to the staff members on the leader page and in the input section with whom I usually deal. I thank too Marilyn Warnick and the marketing staff for their co-operation in this publication, "in association with *The Daily Telegraph*".

To have been allowed to effect this ministry in print in such a great national newspaper is, I repeat, an immense privilege. To have the Meditations reaching yet further out into the world is a happy but humbling thought. I hope someone, somewhere, will find them a blessing.

June 1994   Denis Duncan

Be Still and Know. . .

To be able to be still is to have found the secret of success in the struggle against the strains and stresses of this noisy, raucous and demanding world. It is a capacity made incarnate in the life of our Lord. When faced, as he often was, by criticism, hostility, opposition and, in the end, crucifixion, he never lost his serenity and tranquillity. Even in his darkest hours, he knew how to be still and *know* that God, his Father, was with him in that darkness.

There were times when Jesus's inner peace was severely challenged. In the Garden of Gethsemane, as he sweated blood over the appalling events that faced him; on Calvary, where those events became reality and he was strained to the limit to hold on to his faith and his peace. But he did. The disciple can never emulate the extraordinary spiritual strength of the Master, but the example remains to help us find our peace. We need, like Jesus, to be able, under great pressure, to be still and know that He is God.*

To develop his "still centre", Jesus went to quiet places ... the Mount of Olives, the seashore, the desert place. Paul followed his example. In the desert of Arabia he wrestled with the consequences of the call that came to him on the Damascus Road.

We too must repair to "the desert place" even if, literally, for us that is impossible. It matters not. "The desert place" is the sanctuary we create wherever we are, the place where we can meet God. It may be in the quietness of a church. It may be somewhere in the garden. Perhaps we cannot go anywhere at all through physical limitation, so a corner of a room can be our sanctuary. There, selected symbols will speak to us of spiritual things. It may be simple or splendid, small or large. It is of no importance. "The desert place" is where we meet God in the stillness and know that He is there.

The desert place is also the place where we meet ourselves, where we face the pain of our weakness and our sin. It is here however, that a miracle takes place. It is at the very time when we face ourselves that we know that God is already there, forgiving, redeeming, assuring, renewing. It is in this experience of a loving God that we find the stillness we so eagerly seek.

True serenity comes from knowing God as a living, loving presence. Equipped with such peace, we can face life, a day at a time, with calmness and confidence. Aware of our weakness, physically, emotionally, spiritually, we become the more sure that the divine strength is flowing through our whole being.

Such stillness is not of our making. It is God's gift and it is on offer to all His people.

* *Psalm 46, verse 10* (Psalm numbering throughout the book follows that of The Authorised Version of the Bible)

PART I

SPIRITUAL RESOURCES

Spiritual Resources

"A wider universe demands deeper awareness of the dimension of the spirit and of spiritual resources available for man, of the infinity of God, and of the divine knowledge and understanding still to be claimed." This statement (quoted in Templeton Trust literature) is particularly relevant when set against the materialism that characterises contemporary living. Breadth, depth, development, growth ... these are liberating words and concepts. They contrast starkly with so much that is negative in the world today — declining standards in relationships and behaviour, the constant glorification of the trivial, tunnel vision expressed in narrow views and intolerant attitudes, the selfish individualism that works against real community and social health.

Current political, ethical and even theological confusion is contributing to much of the prevalent "doom and gloom". The gradual removal of what the Old Testament calls "the ancient landmarks" is, metaphorically, affecting public values, personal morality and social standards. Religious people are additionally threatened by the statements of theologians which seem to them to run counter to "all that they must surely believe". And it is all taking place in a world that seems topsy-turvy. Footballers are sold for millions, while starvation reduces its victims to skeletons; the phrase "love child" seems to be reserved for babies born in relationships other than marriage; entertainers and "stars" are celebrated (especially at their deaths) as cult heroes or heroines despite their having lived lives far removed from either the norms of society or from those of the church in particular. No wonder so many feel disillusioned with such a world.

It is imperative, however, that those who strive for better things should lose neither their sense of objectivity nor proportion. The world is, as Gerard Manley Hopkins proclaims it to be, "charged with the grandeur of God!". The amazing beauty, mystery and wonder of creation is revealed to us in ever more dazzling ways by modern technological equipment. In reality, the world is not populated by monsters, murderers, rapists and criminals. It is mostly made up of honest, hard-working and law-abiding people who seek — often against great odds — to create and maintain healthy family life, observe civilised attitudes and value personal loyalty. There is, moreover, a large number of socially responsible human beings, many of them young men and women, whose conscious purpose is to feed the hungry, minister to the sick, look after the old, the frail and the disabled, serve the afflicted; who strive, in sum, to create a better world. So the great unfinished conflict between good and evil goes on. While, in our more depressed moments, it may feel as if evil is triumphant, there is an enormous amount of goodness being fed into the world.

It is essential that people of faith and purpose should not be overwhelmed by (as Paul calls them) "the powers of darkness", the negative forces so present in the atmosphere. That atmosphere needs to be healed by prayer and practical loving. Those who are aware of those "spiritual resources available for human beings", dare not withdraw in disillusionment, from the battle for goodness, beauty and love in this world which in creation was good and which, through grace, can be better.

Creative Silence

"Silence is as deep as Eternity, speech is as shallow as Time." How apposite to any reflection on communication is Thomas Carlyle's comment! He is pointing to a paradox which illuminates the truth, aptly expressed by Christina Rossetti, that silence is "more musical than any song".

"The ministry of silence" has four aspects (at least): the silence we ought to maintain about other people; the silence which is an integral part of prayer ... when we need not to speak, but to listen; the silence of dignity* when the only appropriate answer to abuse is no answer (remembering that Jesus, when faced by his accusers' blasphemies "answered them nothing"); the silence of awe, compelled upon us by the sheer mystery of the divine holiness. How important indeed then is silence to the religious life.

Communication involves the practice of preaching and the ministry of print; healing relationship expressed in a "being with"; the creative arts as instruments of communication to the imagination; the healing ministry, conveying strength and peace to body, soul, mind and spirit. Through each, God makes known His love. There remains however one other way in which truth is learned and grace is given. It is through the power of creative silence.

"That man's silence is wonderful to listen to," said Thomas Hardy. Consider then just how much can be said by silence ... the sympathy that silence can convey when, in situations of tragedy and loss, words fail completely; the inner wonder experienced in the contemplation of the divine splendour, which "shallow speech" just cannot express; the feeling of being (in the words of the Psalmist) "dumb with silence", faced as we are by the daily horrors of violence, war, destruction, devastation, starvation, wounds and death.

Sometimes only silence can adequately convey our inner feelings.

In this noisy, tumultuous world, it is right to remember the prayer expressed by Edmund Hamilton Sears

> *O hush the noise, ye men of strife*
> *and hear the angels sing.*

God is in the silence of "the desert place". It is there that we come to know ourselves. It is there that He meets with us. The revelation of the forgiving, renewing love of God in "the silence of eternity" makes it indeed a truly creative silence.

* This theme is developed in *The Silence of Dignity*, Number 50

Comfortable Words

Every act of worship, William Barclay tells us, should include the note of comfort. "Comfort ye, comfort ye my people." "Comfortable words" as I understand them, are not only soothing, calming, restful words but — more importantly, as the Latin root *fortis* in the word "comfort" implies — fortifying, reassuring, encouraging words. The consequences of the proclamation of the Gospel should be positive, enlivening and enhancing for the "Good News" it brings is not negative, discouraging or judgmental.

John's Gospel affirms the *positive* purpose of the Word: "God sent not his Son into the world to condemn the world, but that the world through him might be saved". The Incarnation was a positive action which offered the opportunity for relationships with God to be restored, an offer made to all who choose to receive it. It is not surprising that, in Jesus's farewell message to his disciples, he promised to send them "another Comforter". That was and is the Holy Spirit.

Be it in the older traditional vocabulary of justification and sanctification; in the biblical language of salvation and "fruits of the Spirit"; in contemporary words such as wholeness and growth, the thrust is the same. The divine initiatives in the scheme of redemption all seek to create purpose, meaning, reconciliation and peace. How beautifully *The Book of Common Prayer* sums it up: "Hear what comfortable words our Saviour Jesus Christ saith to all that truly turn to him".

The words that I have used so far are almost all from the New Testament, but the storehouse of encouraging words for the development of the spiritual and devotional life must surely be the Old Testament psalms. I find the practice, suggested by a spiritual director, of underlining in red particularly significant phrases and sentences very helpful. It may be a familiar phrase from Psalm 23 such as "He restoreth my soul" or the opening words of Psalm 46: "God is our refuge and strength, a very present help in trouble". It may be the anguished cry brought about by trial or tribulation: "Out of the depths have I cried to thee, O Lord: Lord, hear my voice" (Psalm 130), or the reminder of the ever-watchful Providence: "He that keepeth thee will not slumber" (Psalm 121). It may be the reassuring statement from Psalm 125 that recalls "the eternal verities": "They that trust in the Lord shall be as Mount Zion which cannot be removed but abideth for ever".

The Psalms persistently point to the Providence of God as a fundamental article of faith. It is not, however, a conviction reached primarily by intellectual endeavour. It is presented as the result of experience, both in the history of God's people and the stories of individual lives. The same conviction is classically stated in Paul's second letter to Timothy: "I know whom I have believed and am persuaded that he is able to keep that which I have committed unto him". With hindsight, as people of faith look back on life's aspects of joy, anguish or pain, they can begin both to see and say, as they could not at the time of their tragedies: "All things (can) work together for good" for those who serve and love their Lord.

It is the experience of God in creation and redemption which is reflected in the comfortable words that fortify and reassure the soul, strengthen the body, bring serenity to the mind and satisfy the heart.

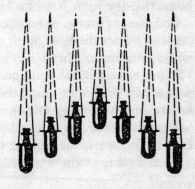

Waiting for God

For those who are emotionally and nervously exhausted, the first needs may well be rest and food. It is not sensible to make demanding decisions when we are physically worn out.

This certainly seems to be the message coming from the story (in I Kings, chapter 19) of the prophet Elijah's deep depression. Hounded by the prophets of Baal, facing the faithlessness and consequent hostility of the children of Israel, and having to fight for God totally alone, Elijah felt compelled to cry out: "I've had enough, Lord. Please take away my life". Wearied to death, he was asleep under a juniper tree when a ministering angel brought him food and drink. "Arise and eat," the angel said. Only then was Elijah ready to face the deep spiritual issues before him.

It was, however, precisely as he waited on God that he "got it all wrong". It was in the dramatic and the extraordinary that God would presumably make Himself known. God was not, however, in the rushing wind, the cataclysmic earthquake or the scorching fire. What Elijah must do was simple: just listen to "the still, small voice".

There is a reminder of this selfsame spiritual law in the story of the walk to Emmaus. It was in the commonplace process of "breaking bread" at an *ordinary* meal in an *ordinary* home that the risen Jesus made himself known.

God does, of course, sometimes reveal Himself in dramatic events. Did not the Holy Spirit come, at the first Pentecost, with a "rushing, mighty wind" and "tongues of fire"? There was, too, an earthquake at the precise moment that Jesus died on Calvary. But more often the Divine presence is made known in the everyday events of life — family, fellowship, loving relationship, quiet reflection, silent contemplation, the care of the carers, the courage of the strugglers.

He is there in forgiveness and encouragement when people

fail. Was it not to Peter, who denied him, that Jesus wanted news of his resurrection sent? Was it not to Thomas who doubted him that he showed his pierced hands? It was to those same disciples who had "forsaken him and fled" that the Holy Spirit was given.

Seeking for God in the unusual can be a temptation — Jesus himself had to reject that very subtle pressure when he was "tempted of the devil". Finding Jesus in the commonplace was the blessing that came to the two who walked to Emmaus. So can it be for us all.

For further comments on the walk to Emmaus, see *Emmaus Encounter*, Number 6; *Transforming Vision*, Number 7; *Preparing the Way*, Number 8

Emmaus Encounter

In Luke's Gospel there is the dramatic resurrection story which we know as "The Walk to Emmaus". It is profoundly moving in its demonstration of the reality and validity of spiritual experience but, because it is concerned with contemporary concepts such as changes to consciousness and levels of awareness, it is also very relevant today. The changes to which it bears witness are not, however, artificially created or drug induced. They are wholly the product of an encounter with the risen Christ.

Two followers, as they walked, had "reasoned together" about events that had taken place in Jerusalem relating to Jesus of Nazareth. As they told the stranger who joined them on their journey, they had been discussing his crucifixion and reports of his resurrection, yet even when he expounded their scriptures with authority they were completely unaware of his identity.

A little later on, as they shared their evening meal with the stranger, something happened that transformed their spiritual awareness. "Their eyes were opened," we read, "and they knew him". Returning to Jerusalem, they reported to the assembled disciples that the stranger, the risen Jesus, had been made known to them "in breaking of bread".

Symbols and rituals play an important part in everyday life. To the development of the spiritual life of the individual and of the church, they are even more important. They are, however, means, not ends in themselves. When they become ends, they lose their purpose. Rightly used, they are aids to the growth of the spiritual life, for they become the point around which images and beliefs cluster.

The symbol has a special power. It is the ability to bring into consciousness the great themes gathered around it. To contemplate the symbol of the cross is immediately to be reminded of God's saving acts through the crucifixion and resurrection of Jesus.

Breaking of bread was a normal, natural action within that meal, but it was profoundly symbolic too. It brought flooding into the consciousness of the two followers that other meal in an upper room where Jesus shared with his friends not only his coming death and resurrection, but himself. So meaningful was the action that "their eyes were opened" and their level of awareness dramatically raised. They recognised their Lord.

The Emmaus experience lies beyond our reach, but through prayer, meditation and contemplation, our level of spiritual awareness can change too, and enable us to "touch and handle things unseen".

27

Transforming Vision

"Why do you stand there, gazing up to heaven?" There is an implied rebuke in the question put to the disciples on the first Ascension Day by "two men in white apparel". Surely they know that, as he promised, he will "in like manner", come again. It is time to stop gazing heavenwards, come down to earth and go back to work for his Kingdom.

There is a place in religious life for both contemplation and activity. If, however, involvement in the world "in his name" is to be effective, it must be founded on vision. Faith without works easily becomes false piety. Activity without faith is no more than useful service.

The two followers on their journey to Emmaus, experienced a heightened level of spiritual awareness. As we have noted earlier, through the symbol of "breaking of bread" they became conscious of the presence of the risen Lord. He had joined them on their walk, an unrecognised stranger who had expounded the scriptures to them. In a moment of evening wonder, they recognised the risen Christ.

It was a combination of circumstances that created the context in which the miracle was possible. As the three men approached Emmaus, night began to fall. With traditional hospitality the two followers invited "the stranger" to stay the night. He, however, "made as if he would go further", but they "constrained" him, insisting that he would tarry with them. It was that insistence that led to the situation in which the miracle could occur. So overwhelmed were the two men by what had happened to them that they immediately returned to Jerusalem to share the news of Jesus's resurrection with the apostles.

Mystic experience cannot be achieved, only received. It is, nevertheless, open to all who humbly seek and reverently ask, to be allowed as I said before to "touch and handle things unseen". Circumstances can then combine, in spiritual synchronicity, to open the way for a transforming vision.

It may come in an act of worship; in the solitude of the mountain top; in the serenity of green pastures and by still waters; in the awesome holiness of some silent sanctuary; in an intimate relationship with a loved one; in "the desert place" where we meet with God and with ourselves. However momentary the experience, the result is grace and renewal ... as the transforming vision surely was for the two who walked to Emmaus.

Preparing the Way

Worship involves every aspect of our being, physical, mental, emotional and spiritual. It dare not be treated as if it were simply an intellectual exercise nor should it be turned into merely an emotional indulgence. Both intellect and emotions are, of course, involved.

It is sad when deep emotional needs, such as grieving, are not met in worship. Equally, of course, the body should have an opportunity in worship for the expression of celebration and joy. "Dancing in the aisles", an ancient as well as a modern religious activity, will appeal to some but not to all. It does, however, allow physical expression to worship. The fundamental point is the need for body, soul, mind and emotions all to be embraced in worship together.

I return to the story of the walk to Emmaus for it contains "a cautionary tale" of some importance. The two followers of Jesus, were "reasoning together" about religious matters. They were, in fact, discussing the crucifixion and reported resurrection of Jesus when "the stranger" joined them and expounded the scriptures to them. Amazingly, though they were engaged in theological discussion about Jesus, they were totally blind as to who he actually was. That was indeed strange.

This is not a condemnation of theological debate. There is a need for more theology in the churches today, not less. It is simply a warning that we can discuss the great saving acts of Jesus intellectually but have no sense of the reality of his risen presence.

In worship, similarly, we can do all the technically right things, minds concentrated, emotions stimulated, but however correct our religious behaviour, if we are not aware of the Christ "in the midst", the basic purpose of worship has been missing, to our spiritual loss. Worship is the experience of a loving and "grace-full" relationship with Christ. It is his promise that where two or three — or more — gather together "in his name", he is there to meet with, and minister to, them.

Those who lead worship have a great responsibility, for they are asked to create the ambience in which the Lord may meet with, and minister to, people. Every item in an act of worship — praise, prayers, readings, sermon — must contribute to the transforming encounter with the risen Christ.

To lead worship is to have the privilege of "preparing the way of the Lord".

Devotional Discipline

James S Stewart was a prince among preachers. Whenever
it was made known — in the Forties, Fifties and Sixties —
that he would be in a particular pulpit, the crowds would
gather, not in the sermon-tasting context of other years, but
simply to hear his profound biblical exposition and its
penetrating application to life. Although he spent the later
part of his ministry as an academic — he taught New
Testament language and literature in the Faculty of Divinity
in Edinburgh University — he always remained the
quintessential pastor and preacher. An exceptionally shy man
(as some of the best pastors are), his genuine saintliness
showed itself in the quality of his personal ministry and the
manifest strength of his disciplined devotional life.

In discussing that necessary element of discipline in the
spiritual life, I take very seriously Augustine's cautionary
word: "He is a vain preacher of the word of God without,
who is not a hearer within". To that I say "Amen". None
of us finds it easy to be devotionally disciplined.

When writing (in 1980) a devotional book of prayers and
thoughts for each day called A Day at a Time, I asked James
Stewart, whom I had known for many years, about his
devotional discipline. With typical graciousness, he shared
his practice with me.

Before prayers in the morning, he read (1) a lectionary
passage from the Bible; (2) an excerpt from Pray Today,
published by his church and mine, The Church of Scotland;
(3) the appropriate reading from "my father's well-thumbed
copy" of Daily Light; and (4) a section from the late John
Baillie's A Diary of Private Prayer. After evening prayers, he
used three aids — first something from the Upper Room;
secondly, one of the Psalms, and finally a chapter from a
specifically devotional writer (he gave Evelyn Underhill as an

example). This may feel to be a rather demanding devotional programme — and a little dated — but it indicates the sort of spiritual exercise to which we could usefully aspire. In the end, of course, *our* programme must be matched to *our* needs.

Religious, that is monks and nuns, live "in community" and therefore have the benefit of a devotional structure to help them maintain their spiritual priorities. One of the pleasures of being at Taizé was the sound of the bells regularly summoning all, community members and visitors alike, to prayer. In the ordinary world, it is less easy to give a proper priority to devotional obligations. Time, duties, business pressures, responsibilities, anxieties, lack of energy, can combine to prevent consistency in the spiritual life; yet deep down we know that there cannot be a living faith if the needs of the inner being are ignored and the means of grace neglected.

"Time set aside for the inner life is an essential part of our spiritual development," says my friend and colleague, Dr Martin Israel, pathologist and now priest. The late Christopher Bryant writes encouragingly: "It is of great importance to persevere with set times of prayer and not give up". The form, length and content of our spiritual exercises must be our own. There is certainly, Jesus tells us, no need for "much speaking". Long or short, articulate or inarticulate, what really matters is that our worship is from the heart. But that devotion will always be enhanced by the exercise of discipline.

Little Miracles

It was from a hill above Tiberias that I first had sight of the Sea of Galilee. There, in reality, was the stretch of water of which I had heard and read since Sunday School days. It was deeply moving, for was it not round these shores that Jesus had walked and talked, preached and healed? And, of course, it was the water on which, on a stormy night, he had so dramatically walked.

It is not really necessary to try to explain rationally this, or any other, miracle. The story is a record of the disciples' *experience*. Significantly it is present in all four Gospels. And as one of them notes, so traumatic was the effect of Jesus's presence and actions that it reinforced their awareness of his divinity.

Miracles are, as the Latin derivation of the word indicates, "wonder-full" happenings. If, however, it feels difficult to accept the miraculous element, look on the story as a teaching parable and you will find it points to familiar but important aspects of Jesus's ministry and teaching. Then because disciples "must be as their Master", it follows that his approaches to ministry must be made incarnate in his church, the healing community, too.

First, Jesus comes to frightened men with a *calming word*. "It is I! Be not afraid!". 3am is — especially for the sleepless, the anxious, the fearful, the doubting and those distressed by guilt — the darkest hour. It was, in fact, in "the fourth watch" that Jesus came to still the storms, internal as well as external. That, the distinguished New Testament scholar and my student colleague of long ago, Dr Robin Wilson, tells us "would be about 3am"*. The calming word comes in the darkest hour. May the healing community continue to convey that blessing to anxious people.

Second, Jesus stretched out to frightened Peter, faithless

and sinking, a *helping hand*. Those who choose to follow the one who stilled the storm must constitute themselves not only the *worshipping* community, but also the *serving* community. This, theologically, the doctrine of the Incarnation compels. That service includes, of course, the personal helping hand, but must be expressed in a total involvement in the life of the world, its pain, its poverty, its problems and its politics. For what is politics but the discipline that deals with human concerns, the people's health and homes, education, social welfare, personal needs?

Third, it was the *lack of faith* on the part of the disciples that most concerned Jesus. He spoke in terms of the need to have faith that would "move mountains", but the level of his expectation was too high for his disciples. Not surprisingly, it is for most of us. Bitter experience, unanswered (as we feel it) prayer, overwhelming suffering, bereavement and/or perhaps rejection may have created the crisis of faith and doubt which leaves us with the "little faith" which Jesus so often found around him. In the sophisticated, materialistic world of today, simple faith feels facile and the so-called power of prayer irrelevant. And yet there are those like the little crippled lady who spoke to me after the service on Sunday about each day's "little miracles".

"Be not faithless, but believing," said Jesus to his disciples then, and he says it still. It is a tough demand. But taken seriously, as the Lord's commands must be, little miracles may well come.

* Commentary on the *Gospel of St Mark* In Peake's *Commentary on the Bible* (Thomas Nelson)

The Eternal Verities

"How shall they hear without a preacher?" Paul asks the Romans. "Here am I, send me," was the prophet Isaiah's response to a similar question. Prophets, priests and preachers are among those who have responded to the call to communicate the unchanging Word to a constantly changing world.

The proclamation of "the eternal verities" must relate to the location, culture and time-setting of those to whom it is addressed. Ways have to be found to convey the great truths of the faith ... the offer of a right relationship with God, the assurance of forgiveness, the promise of new life ... in a way that will be understood.

When I first came to live in London, I found myself using phrases from my Scottish background which completely puzzled those to whom I spoke. "I am going to get the messages," I would say, only to encounter blank looks. Had I said instead: "I am going to do the shopping," there would have been no problem. The basic fact was the same, but it had to be expressed in a way comprehensible to people in another cultural context.

The New Testament demonstrates superbly the way in which these "eternal verities" can reach very different people. The essential truth which the Gospel proclaims is that, through Jesus Christ, the restoration of a right relationship with God becomes possible. The concepts and words in which this truth is conveyed vary greatly — "entering the Kingdom", "receiving eternal life", "salvation", "redemption", etc.

It would be naïve to say that each of these words or phrases means exactly the same, for much academic discussion would be involved in expounding their history and precise meaning. What I seek to show is simply that the great truths must be described in different ways depending on the background, interests and history of those to whom they are presented. To one group one of these words or phrases will be meaningless, but to another dynamite — and *vice versa*.

What are the concepts to which we need to turn to be relevant today? Surely to words such as meaning, purpose, reconciliation, relationship. The world is confused by cults and theories, devastated by suffering (and suffering always raises the most difficult questions), depressed by feelings of meaninglessness and purposelessness. The Gospel message must be a giving of wholeness to, and a reason for, life. God offers the possibility of inner peace through the finding of a purpose. Restored relationship with God will transform all other relationships — to others, to the earth, to our inner selves. In a world too often trivial and tawdry, a world of inner despair and outward devastation, a world increasingly devoid of the sense of the numinous, the faith must continue to be proclaimed — but never with arrogance, always with humility.

Of Little Faith

Many find it hard these days to adhere to Jesus's exhortation "to take no anxious thought for tomorrow". Our world, obsessed by the need for security at one level, is at other levels incredibly insecure. "Few people in the work place, from the most senior to the most junior, now have security of employment" claims the Industrial Committee of The Church of Scotland in its report to the General Assembly. It goes on: "Security of work has become a casualty in the last ten years or so". That insecurity leads to financial insecurity, which in turn creates mental and emotional insecurity. The result is widespread stress. It needs a strong faith to cope with life's pressures today. But even those with a real sense of spiritual security must find it hard not to be anxious about the future.

There are religious people who feel guilty because they cannot muster a proper degree of faith. Devout Christians will particularly worry about the dilemma because of the import of the Gospel message about faith and faithlessness. Those "of little faith" are sternly rebuked by Jesus. When Peter, walking on the water towards Jesus, began to sink he found the low level of his faith to be blamed. The disciples, petrified by the storm, are asked: "How is it that you have not faith?". When the disciples cannot cure a boy with epilepsy it is associated with the failures of a "faithless and perverse generation". Highly commended by Jesus, on the other hand, are people of admirable faith — those who brought the man who was "sick of the palsy", the Canaanite woman who pleaded for her daughter's healing; the one Samaritan leper who returned to give thanks; the woman with the haemorrhage. Is it then just a matter of simple faith and all will be truly well? A priest I knew, a saintly man, died broken and bitter because he had all the faith possible for one human being, but he was not healed. There are many like that.

Our uncertainty increases when we read in the letter of James that "faith without works is dead". He writes pragmatically: "Suppose a fellowman or woman has not clothes to wear and no food for a daily meal, and suppose one of you says in such a situation: 'Go, and God bless you! May you have a fire to warm yourself and a meal to eat'. And suppose you do not give that person enough to keep body and soul together, what use is that? If faith does not issue in action, if it is all alone by itself, it is dead".* The exhortation to "have faith in God" can, alas, seem no more than empty religious words to the starving, the unemployed, the poor, the bruised and battered of society.

But still that sense of unease about being of little faith remains. Indeed it will be increased when we look at homes of loving like William Quarrier's Homes in Bridge of Weir (to name but one). Founded on faith, operated in faith, Quarrier's makes its needs known and leaves the rest in God's hands. God has marvellously honoured its faith. Are we too often of too little faith?

* *William Barclay's Translation of the New Testament* (Arthur James)

True Humility

The moment I entered the room at Quarrier's Homes, I realised that I was in the presence of true greatness. There stood a little man who had a reputation worldwide for his witness and his work. His ministry was to proclaim the Christian message in the slums of Kobe in Japan, but it was for more than that that his name was held in honour. Toyohiko Kagawa had always incarnated his message in his offering of loving care to the poor, the sick, the destitute and the dying. Despite his own serious illnesses and frequent weakness, he had never ceased to give himself totally to the people whom, in Christ's name, he loved. In our brief conversation, I was so aware that the greatness of this man lay not in his fame but in his humility.

"There's nothing so becomes a man as modest stillness and humility" — at least in times of peace, said Shakespeare (in *Henry V*). There is certainly no quality so deeply rooted in the New Testament as true humility. Paul writing to the Philippians, explains why this is so. "It would have been no robbery," for Jesus to have "claimed equality with God", but what in fact did he do? "He made himself of no reputation and took upon himself the form of a servant, and was made in the likeness of men". But there is more. "Being found in fashion as a man, he humbled himself and became obedient unto death, even the death of the cross." There is no doubt as to the implications of this for his followers. Paul puts it clearly: "Let this mind be in you which was also in Christ Jesus". Christians are called to don "the garment of humility".

There is no place for arrogance in either individual or corporate religion but, for individuals and groups alike, this is a hard undertaking. Was not arrogance the primal sin in the Garden of Eden? Adam and Eve, our representatives, wanted to be "like God".

It is humility, not arrogance, that will win not only the attention of the world, but also its heart. The harvest of the Spirit was evidenced in the life of Kagawa by the power of his humility. So must it be with us all.

The Turning-point

I can still see the picture in my mind's eye although it happened so long ago. There was the great American theologian Reinhold Niebuhr, moved to mirth at the sight of his old friend and my teacher, John Baillie, in the quaint breeches and related garb worn by Moderators of the General Assembly of the Church of Scotland in their year of office. It was the light moment in an after-dinner speech, restricted to seven minutes, in which Niebuhr offered the most profoundly moving analysis of "the human dilemma". This, as I recall his words, could not be resolved by philosophy however profound, by education however intensive, by scientific progress however dramatic or by psychological understanding however acute. There was only one answer to the depth of human need and that was "the grace of our Lord Jesus Christ".

The Gospel proclaims that fundamental inner change is needed if new life is to be found. "Except you be converted ..." said Jesus, "you cannot enter the Kingdom". When speaking with Nicodemus, he called it being "born again". Conversion is then a necessary experience but, unfortunately, the word itself is often interpreted in too limited a way. As a result, it tends to divide rather than unite, and that is sad indeed.

There is no need for such conflict. The word "conversion", by derivation, means "turning-point". An experience of inner transformation is a step on the way to salvation. *It is however, the experience itself which is mandatory, not the way in which it happens.* For, just as there is diversity in the gifts of the Spirit, so there are various ways by which God brings about inner change.

"Youth is the time to go flashing from one side of the world to the other, both in mind and body; to try the manners of different nations; to hear the chimes at midnight; to see sunrise in town and country, to be converted at a revival ..." says Robert Louis Stevenson in *Crabbed Age and Youth*. But this seems to limit conversion to a "revivalist" experience and to "the age of adolescence". It can be both, but it need not be either!

Inner transformation does take place at crusades, in mission halls, within the church, in that dramatic, public way that can be timed and dated. There are many admirable people who have been "saved", "born again", charismatically renewed in such circumstances. But there are others who have experienced "the miracle of grace" in less emotional, less traumatic, less public but equally convincing ways. There is a group — and John Baillie was one of them — who, as he commented, had never known a time because of their upbringing by devout parents "when Jesus was not my Lord". For them, confirmation of their baptismal vows and public affirmation was and is their transforming experience.

An adolescent experience? Yes, such a turning-point often is. But midlife crisis, as Jungian thought confirms, can also be the occasion for fundamental redirection. It is the time when spiritual, creative life often emerges, and the movement towards integration develops. This too is a miracle of grace.

When a prodigal son returned transformed, there was spontaneous joy, and rightly so. This — and not controversy about how it happens — is the appropriate response when someone "was lost and is found".

43

Miracle of Grace

Don't expect miracles if you are over 40! That seems to be the message coming from Luke's report (in the Acts of the Apostles) of the disciples' healing of the lame man. The wonder of the miracle was even greater, Luke notes (and significantly he was a doctor by profession) because "the man was over 40 years old, on whom this miracle of healing was shewed". We now believe, of course, in the good news that "life begins at 40" — or, for that matter, 50 or 60. There is always the possibility of change and growth. Call the experience what you will — inner transformation, interior change, conversion, the turning-point — it can come at any age.

It is the second half of life which is the potentially creative half. The pressures arising from the making of a career, the securing of a home, the education and care of the family, dominate the first half of life. After 40, roughly speaking, there is more likely to be time available to explore undeveloped parts of our being and release the creative potential all too often dammed up by material pursuits.

Alas, in today's world, this is more a statement of the ideal than a reflection of reality for too many people. So many nowadays, both the young and the middle-aged, have no careers to create. There are no jobs for the redundant over-fifties. There is no relief from the pressures of the rat-race. We must not, however, allow the ideal to fade away or the creative potential of life to be swamped. Indeed there are many still who find that in mid-life, crisis can be an opportunity. Life can be transformed. Gifts can be discovered. Creative self-awareness can develop. It is a time to grow. Those who do not proclaim a religious faith will see in such creativity indicators on the road to maturity or, as Jung called it, individuation. Those for whom faith is an essential part of life will see constructive inner change as evidence of the Spirit at work in the miracle of grace.

The conversion of Paul, formerly persecutor of the church, finally "the least of the apostles", is, in terms of transformation experience, an interesting and helpful model. His Damascus Road encounter must seem to many the prime example of a timed and dated conversion experience, whereas in fact the whole process took time. Outwardly aggressive, he "breathes out threatenings and slaughter against the disciples of the Lord". Inwardly the challenge to his conscience is taking place. Was it that he knew he was wrong to "consent" to the stoning of the martyr Stephen? In the words of William Barclay, Paul actually "thoroughly approved" of Stephen's murder. Did not unconscious feelings of guilt move him in the heat of the midday sun towards that hysterical collapse and blindness, the crisis in which he encountered the Jesus whom he persecuted? But more time was needed — three days — and then God sends to him a somewhat trembling but devout spiritual counsellor. Ananias laid hands on God's "chosen vessel". The gift of the Spirit was Paul's.

Challenge, crisis, change ... for some it happens in a minute, for others it may need months, perhaps even a lifetime. But the miracle of grace can come at any time. And it can certainly happen to the over-forties!

Absolute Demand

Those who claim that the Church should be more "in tune with the times" seem to imply that, by accommodating the Gospel to today's needs, the faith becomes more "attractive". There is however little evidence that, by making entry to the Christian life easier, the number of those who come into the church is likely to increase. The reverse is, in fact, closer to the truth. It is in the churches that emphasise the *demand* of the Gospel that growth shows most clearly.

Jesus, in his attitude to life and to people, made clear the "absolute demand" (to use a phrase from the late Professor H H Farmer) of the Gospel. Those who love father, mother, son or daughter "more than me" said Jesus are "not worthy of me". Discipleship means "leaving all", "taking up the Cross" and following him.

Jesus asked much of his disciples, but he founded the "absolute demand" which he made on them on his own acceptance of that demand by himself. This commitment he expressed in his attitude to his coming death. Luke tells us that he "steadfastly set his face to go to Jerusalem", knowing the consequences. He had, he said, to do the will of the Father who sent him. While in the Garden of Gethsemane, the human part of him rebelled at the suffering he had to face ("if it be possible, let this cup pass from me"), the "absolute demand" that was involved in fulfilling "the will of my Father" compelled him to add: "Nevertheless, not my will but thine be done".

The language of faith has many words in its vocabulary that remind us of the *corporate* nature of Christianity ... community, congregation, fellowship, kingdom, body, etc. Remembering that basic aspect of the church will help to prevent any over-emphasis on individualism in religion. That said, however, personal obedience remains an absolute demand from which no follower can claim exception.

Jesus, in declaring his own attitude to life, asks his disciples to reflect his lifestyle. It is one in which there is an absolute demand to "seek first the Kingdom" and let all other things fall into their proper place. It was to Peter, concerning himself with what would happen to another disciple in the future, that Jesus's demand was made crystal clear. "Peter," he said in effect, "don't worry about what is to happen to others. *You follow me!*"

Half and Half

What a glorious book is that of the Old Testament prophet, Ezekiel. No wonder my old Principal in New College, Edinburgh — the late Professor W A Curtis — advised us all to give it very special attention. It is the book which gives the most accurate definition possible of a healing, pastoral or counselling relationship: "I sat where they sat". It is the book which offers that dramatic death and resurrection story, the utter desolation of the valley of dry bones transformed into new life by the inspiration of God's spirit. It is the book which, particularly in the *New English Bible* translation, presents the most remarkably tender picture of the infinitely caring love of God: "I myself will tend my flock, I myself pen them in their fold, says the Lord God. I will search for the lost, recover the straggler, bandage the hurt ...". It is the book in which this same God "sought for a man among them that should ... stand in the gap" for Him, only for the sad, bathetic "punchline" to follow: "But I found none".

The God of Ezekiel is a God of huge tenderness and infinite loving-kindness, but He is also the God who makes that "absolute demand" to which I have referred in the previous meditation. The demand is for nothing less than complete commitment. The demand is echoed in the New Testament in the words of Jesus to actual and potential disciples "Whosoever will come after me, let him deny himself, take up his cross and follow me".

There is a fascinating translation of Psalm 119, verse 113, in one of the early "new translations", that greatly respected one by James Moffatt. It runs: "I hate men who are *half and half*". That is a clear statement about failure in individual commitment. Corporate failure is equally condemned in one of the letters to the seven churches at the beginning of the book of Revelation. The language is strong and the condemnation devastating, leaving the church of the Laodiceans in no doubt of the divine view of failure in commitment: "I know thy works, that thou art neither cold nor hot. So then because thou art lukewarm, and neither cold nor hot, I will spit you out of my mouth".

Commitment, if willingly and voluntarily given to a proper cause or a leader of integrity, is a great gift. But the choice of the subject or object of commitment is crucial. Directed to a wrong cause or a flawed leader, such blind commitment turns into fanaticism. The results of that are all too visible in the world today … terrorism, persistence in violence and war whatever suffering they bring to the innocent. The world has suffered too much from uncritical adherence to destructive activity for false motives.

There is no doubt, however, of the value of commitment for religious faith so long as it is freely and responsibly made, objectively understood and enthusiastically offered. Alas, it was just this which the admirably honest, rich young ruler could not give, departing sorrowfully as a result. This, too made King Agrippa's comment to Paul interesting in its context but ultimately irrelevant. "Almost," he said, "thou persuadest me to be a Christian". But "almost" and "commitment" bear no relation to each other. Half-and-half people will never make disciples.

The Power of Prayer

"To travel hopefully is a better thing than to arrive," wrote Robert Louis Stevenson. The religious journey has something of this "feel" about it. It is not that spiritual goals are unimportant, of course, but the great blessing is really to know that you are travelling in the right direction.

If this is true for individual pilgrimages, it applies to corporate situations too. "Where there is no vision, the people perish," it says in the book of Proverbs. Where there is no sense of direction in events, the same is true. How desperately we all try to see the right direction for the greater peace of what used to be Yugoslavia, but confusion and contumacy reign. In Ireland over the years of the Troubles, direction has been lost in sectarian feuds and traditional but unquestioned religious hostility. There was a sense of puzzlement throughout the nation on a certain Wednesday when interest rates went up and down in rapid but perplexing succession. Had we lost our economic direction? When we lose our way in both personal and corporate situations, we can experience a lostness and a meaninglessness that is devastating.

There was a time when Mary Magdalene found herself looking in the wrong direction. Her weeping eyes were focused on the tomb and her missing Lord. Then she turned round and, looking in the other direction, she found herself face to face with the living Lord. This was a turning-point indeed for Mary.

One of the "eternal verities" is the belief that God's grace and power can completely change the direction of lives. "I met a man," said the late and great Dr John White, referring to his encounter with Jesus. That was the secret of his robust conviction. The vocabulary of faith includes, as I have said before, words such as renewal, regeneration, redemption and reconciliation. They testify to the fact that, through grace, everything can change — aims, attitudes, reactions, relationships, even indeed our whole philosophy of life.

Change is the action of God, but Jesus encouraged and indeed commanded his followers to contribute to the possibility of change in people and in situations by importunate prayer. "The prayer of a good man is powerfully effective," said James, as is equally the prayer of a good woman. Intercessory prayer is the process through which we co-operate with God in bringing about change, in providing direction.

No wonder Paul says to the Thessalonians: "Pray without ceasing," or Tennyson to us all, "More things are wrought by prayer than this world dreams of".

The Validity of Prayer

There is a need for discipline in prayer but is prayer itself relevant to today's, and tomorrow's, world? Increasingly, the number diminishes of those who believe, with James (in his New Testament letter), that "effectual fervent prayer ... availeth much". It is another part of the crisis of faith and doubt that is affecting the church corporately and people individually.

There are several reasons for the diminishing belief in prayer. Some are intellectual, some psychological and some circumstantial. Intellectually, many find the traditional concepts of the transcendent God "out there" no longer tenable and turn, as the much-publicised case of an Anglican priest facing such a crisis did, to what he called "Christian humanism". Emotionally, rejection by a loved one may destroy that other relationship of love, relationship with God. Circumstantially, the pressure to set aside faith may come most of all from reaction to the suffering of the world. More and more, the critic's question — "Why does God allow such suffering?" — becomes the believer's question too. Why has the God who, through grace, is the author of change, not dealt positively with the dreadful pain of starving, violated, damaged people?

The validity of prayer, and the particular form of it known as intercession, cannot be established on a purely intellectual basis. That is not to say, for one moment, that intellectual reflection is valueless. It is imperative that great intellects continue to reflect on the basic material of the faith. But while reflection on the material of the faith is essential, the material itself — the eternal verities — is not intellectually conceived. It belongs to what Paul called, in a profound sentence in his letter to the Ephesians, the knowledge which is beyond knowledge. It is in that second dimension of knowledge that the great mysteries of faith — the miracles of incarnation and resurrection — lie. Jesus testified to this in his response to Peter's confession of his Messiahship when he affirmed that Peter's spiritual perception was not revealed by "flesh and blood" but was given "by my Father which is in heaven". Prayer belongs to that dimension. Its validity is not established by mental gymnastics but by spiritual perceptiveness. If belief in the efficacy of prayer has fallen victim to the crisis of faith and doubt, the need is not for increased academic and intellectual effort but for a renewal of inner vision.

The discipline of prayer is vigorously encouraged by Jesus who specifically says "Ask … Seek … Knock …", who commends the "friend at midnight" who pleads his cause to the point of nuisance but receives the answer he needs. If Jesus is the authority in matters spiritual and the Lord who demands obedience, there is no possibility of setting aside prayer as irrelevant. It was the "firm foundation" of his life and he expects his followers to make it that too.

The validity and efficacy of prayer depends not on our weak faith, but on God's providence and grace. When, damaged by doubt, faith falters and fails; when perhaps because of tragedy, spiritual sensitivity becomes numb; when the divine presence feels distant — as it has done for many a saint — it is essential to remember that it is not our frail grasp of God that is important, but his "mighty grasp" of us.* We are in the embrace of a love that simply will not let us go.

* These lines are quoted in *The Healing Light*, Number 88

Co-operators with God

"I sought for a man among them that would stand in the gap ... but I found none." The failure and faithlessness of chosen people is a constant theme in the Old Testament. It persists, too, in the New Testament. As the death of Jesus drew nearer, Judas betrayed him, Peter denied him and "all the disciples forsook him and fled".

To over-emphasise this somewhat negative aspect of the relationship between God and His people would, however, be unhelpful. The essence of the divine-human encounter relates to "covenant" and therefore to trust. What is significant is that, despite the persistent tendency of human beings to fail, God chooses to work through them! It is this aspect of co-operation between God and His people that leads Paul to say: "We are workers together with Him". We are co-operators with God.

What, then, is asked of "fellow-workers" who, in the words of God through Ezekiel (quoted at the beginning of this meditation), must "stand in the gap" for him? There are three key concepts.

The first is *conversion*. Some people are uneasy with this word because it is too often associated with a dramatic, emotional, public decision at a particular moment. It is not however the way in which people come to faith that is important. It is the fact itself.

Conversion, by derivation, means "turning-point". For many that turning-point is an affirmation of the faith which has always been theirs. Whatever process we think of as constituting the turning-point in life, the greater need is that we know where we stand as a result of it. That is the first qualification for those who must stand in the gap today.

The second word is *commitment*. Conversion is the beginning of the journey of faith, not the end of it. Lifetime commitment is needed by those who must stand in the gap.

The third word is *concern*. It is not enough to affirm the faith and be committed to it. Discipleship involves both a coming and a going. The coming is to worship and fellowship, but we always come in order to "go into all the world" in service to it.

Converted, committed, concerned are those whom God needs to stand in the gap for Him today. Will He find them?

Creative Discontent

I have some very discontented friends. They are, nevertheless, remarkable people. None of them is content with things as they are, and they are determined to change them. In that lies their courage.

I take one of them as an example, a young woman, Lin Berwick, living a full life.* A trained counsellor and an accredited lay preacher, she specialises in bereavement work and helps disabled people with sexual problems. She lectures, writes books and broadcasts. She has set up a trust to provide holiday homes for people with disabilities. Yet this extraordinary young woman, cerebral-palsied since birth and without the use of the lower part of her body, spends her life in a wheelchair. Moreover, having lost the sight of one eye when she was nine, and the second at 14, she is totally blind. Yet, although so severely handicapped, she has consistently refused to resign herself to the limitations of her position. Her achievements illustrate her determination to change everything she can.

I mention this courageous woman because a statement by Paul in his letter to the Philippians (chapter 4, verse 11), if casually read, may be misleading. He writes: "I have learned in whatsoever state I am therewith to be content".** That sounds very much like resigned acceptance of overwhelming situations. In fact it is not. It is a positive statement about creative discontent. What he is really saying, as he quotes a long list of traumatic events, is this: "In every situation in which I have found myself, I have sought to create opportunity. Within the limitations and hardships of any given set of circumstances, however intolerable, I have found a way to use positively and creatively whatever was happening to me. I have, then, while accepting the things which cannot be changed, found through them true contentment".

"Crisis" in Chinese, is made up of two ideograms. One represents "danger" and the other "opportunity".*** Crises are not pleasant experiences, but they can be doors to growth.

Limitation, hostility and adversity are, spiritually speaking, learning situations. They can develop our inner resources and increase our faith, leading us towards greater maturity. Perhaps the New English Bible's version of Paul's words conveys his intention best: "I have learned to find resources in myself, whatever my circumstances," he says. Then, significantly, he adds: "I have strength for anything through Him who gives me power".

* I refer to Lin again in *Healing through Suffering*, Number 42. Her story is told — by herself — in *Inner Vision* (Arthur James)

** See further reference to this text in *Amazing Grace*, Number 36

*** *See Expectancy*, Number 31

Grapes, Giants and Grasshoppers

The focus in this meditation is on three words: grapes, giants and grasshoppers. The purpose is to encourage the disheartened and support the despairing.

The three words come from the book of Numbers in the Old Testament. The story tells how selected men were sent ahead of the children of Israel to spy out the land of Canaan, given to them by God "to possess it". Two reports were brought back. The first enthused over "the land flowing with milk and honey", and grapes were produced as evidence of its grandeur. The second advised holding back "because there we saw the giants, the sons of Anak, and we were in our own sight as grasshoppers; and so we were in their sight".

Grapes, giants and grasshoppers together symbolise our human problem. The *grapes* represent, as they did for the Israelites, our aims and ideals, our deep-down desires. The *giants* are the threatening obstacles in our way. The *grasshopper* feelings are those of sheer impotence when we are faced by overwhelming odds.

How should we deal with such situations? The story itself (Numbers, chapters 13 and, especially, 14) illustrate possible reactions. The first response (chapter 14, verse 1) is *self-pity*: "and all the congregation lifted up their voice and cried; and the people wept that night". It is a common, human reaction in situations of distress, but it achieves nothing.

The second response (verse 3) is no better. Why has God let this happen to us? "Were it not better to return to Egypt?" It is the *defeatist* reaction. It, too, achieves nothing.

The third response (verse 10) comes after an appeal from the leaders to get up, go on and fight. "But all the congregation bade stone them with stones". *Resentment* is a common reaction to frustration and failure. We put the blame on others but defeat no giants.

The solution of the problem, for the children of Israel, had to come in some other way. It did. The language is religious but the message is clear: "And the glory of the Lord appeared in the tabernacle before all the children of Israel" (verse 10). It was a demonstration of God's presence in power that transformed the people and sent them courageously on.

The biblical message is a consistent one and Jesus repeated it to his disciples: "You shall receive power". Fortified indeed were they for their battle with the giant forces of a hostile world. The promise holds good for all of us. Take courage!

The Gentle Strong

"Meekness," according to Paul, is — like love, joy and peace — evidence of "the fruit of the Spirit" in the Christian life. It is not, however, a word which relates comfortably to the world as we know it. The meek obviously do not "inherit the earth".

It is the word, not the concept, that poses problems. In the Old Testament, the meek are the poor and lowly, a theme which both the New Testament and Jesus continue. "The Son of man hath not where to lay his head," Jesus said. In Paul's great passage on humility in his letter to the Philippians, the stress on self-effacement is added.

In English, meekness is more associated with mildness, and suggests weakness. The "gentle-Jesus-meek-and-mild" image has, however done little to portray effectively the character of Christ or indeed the true ethos of the faith he presented. It is not surprising, therefore, that several translators have looked for words other than meekness in listing evidences of (in William Barclay's phrase) "the harvest of the Spirit". J B Phillips suggests "tolerance" and several versions — for example, *The New English Bible* and *The Jerusalem Bible* — offer "gentleness".

The latter is an improvement, for sensitivity is a valuable and creative quality, but Barclay goes further. Meekness is, rather, "the strength of gentleness". What a marvellous phrase that is, expressing superbly the paradoxical relationship between strength and gentleness! That concept does feel relevant to modern needs, while Shakespeare, too, endorses the theme: "Let gentleness my strong enforcement be" (*As You Like It*).

It is always risky to apply the vocabulary of faith to the somewhat ruthless world of which we are a part. The result may be sentimental or doctrinaire. Reinhold Niebuhr, expounding the theme of his book, *Moral Man and Immoral Society*, pointed to this danger as he emphasised the dominance of power, political, economic and material, in human and especially group relationships.

It is a danger to be taken seriously, but it is not a reason for setting aside spiritual concepts. Change takes place, God declares through the prophet Zechariah, "not by might nor by power, but by my spirit". Jesus, seeking in his religious tradition for a model through which to explain his divine purpose, chose not the warrior king but the suffering servant. It was a choice that set him on the way of the Cross. When, therefore, he entered Jerusalem not on a charger but on an ass, he presented an acted parable about the strength of gentleness.

The Journey of Life

When David Livingstone volunteered for missionary service, he was asked where he was willing to. "I will go anywhere," he replied, "so long as it is forward."

One of the glories of the Christian faith is its offer to all of the possibility of a new beginning. Deep in the heart of most human beings is the desire to "wipe the slate clean", to be forgiven, to be "made new". The doctrine of forgiveness presents that opportunity to all who sincerely seek it.

Jesus made it clear that, where there is genuine penitence, God's forgiveness is total and unconditional. Whatever we have said or done or thought or felt that is unacceptable to Him, to the church, to society or to ourselves is embraced in the miracle of grace and we can go forward with confidence. To engage, then, in continuing self-condemnation, endless recrimination or inappropriate guilt is to deny the forgiveness given and the freedom of spirit received. To know, when we are in deep despair over both our personal failures and the corporate darkness in the world around us, that everything can be made new is the greatest possible encouragement on the spiritual way.

On the journey of life, it is not achievement that matters most; it is sensing that you are travelling in the right direction. Paul had, as he himself claimed, a life that was full of achievements, moral, ethical and religious, but he came to realise — particularly through his experience on the road to Damascus — that he was going in the wrong direction. Conversion was the process by which the whole direction of his life was changed. From then on, he had to "run the race … looking unto Jesus". The secret of success in the spiritual life lies in our ability (as the old chorus says) to "turn your eyes upon Jesus", for he is, in the words of the Letter to the

Hebrews, "the author and finisher of our faith". He gives direction.

"Do you see yonder wicket gate?" asked Evangelist of Christian in John Bunyan's *Pilgrim's Progress*. The answer was "No". Then said Evangelist: "Do you see yonder shining light?" "I think I do," was the reply. Evangelist said: "Keep that light in your eye and go up directly thereto, so shalt thou see the gate; at which when thou knockest, it will be told thee what thou shalt do."

With that light in your eye, in faith, go forward.

Sense of Perspective

What a difference the conjunction "but" can make! It has the capacity to convert a flat statement of fact or opinion into a dramatic declaration of great significance.

Let me illustrate this by quoting one of five "but" statements by Jesus in the Sermon on the Mount. "Ye have heard that it hath been said 'Thou shalt love thy neighbour and hate thine enemy', *but* I say unto you 'Love your enemies, bless them that curse you, do good to them that hate you and pray for them that despitefully use you, and persecute you' ..."

What a powerful point that "but" makes, one that is important as we now reflect on the need for a sense of perspective. There are human perspectives, *but* there is a divine perspective. And they are very different. "My thoughts are not your thoughts," God declares through Isaiah, "neither are your ways my ways."

Paul makes the same kind of point when he stands the human perspective about what is real on its head and emphasises that "the things that are seen" are only ephemeral and "temporal". It is that which is "not seen" which is "eternal". In other words, material things, however important, are nevertheless transitory. It is the invisible spiritual dimension that constitutes ultimate reality. Jesus's point about the priority of "seeking the Kingdom and his righteousness" is another statement of the divine perspective. We human beings invariably demonstrate that it is the "other things" which come first. However important those other things are, it is a false perspective that gives them primary significance.

Spirituality, like holiness, is not expressed in sameness, but in difference; not in closeness to human standards, attitudes and ways but in radically different attitudes. Believers are told by Paul: "Be not conformed to this world, *but* be ye transformed". The doctrine of the Incarnation is a fundamental statement about the total involvement of God in human life and in the life of the world, with all its passion and pain, its trials and temptations, but Jesus still emphasised the stance that disciples must take. Certainly they are *in* the world, but they must not be *of* it.

"There is nothing ugly," said the artist, John Constable, "for let the form of an object be what it may, light, shade and perspective will always make it beautiful." There is something here that feels akin to the Gospel in that, in the divine perspective, every human being, made in the image of God, is of infinite value in His eyes. Humanity may be damaged, *but* there is always on offer the grace that transforms the ugliness of sin into the beauty of holiness. The divine perspective, as a model, may be very demanding, *but* it is never discouraging. Reach for it!

The Right Direction

All that I knew about the hotel in Budapest, to which I was driving from Prague, was its name. It could be anywhere in the city. I spotted a man, standing at a busy junction, studying a map. Extracting myself carefully from the seemingly unending traffic flow, I parked (as others did) on the pavement. Communication, I assumed, would be a problem. In fact, it wasn't. The gentleman was from Croydon. There on his map was the hotel, duly marked, across the river in Pest. I now had my marker and concentrated solely on visualising the most direct route to it; straight to the river, along the bank until you reach a particular bridge, cross the bridge and that road should lead to the hotel. I kept my eye resolutely on the goal, looking at nothing on the way, however potentially interesting. So long as I held to the right direction, I would arrive. I did.

The spiritual life is not a state but a journey. To reach the goal it is essential to ensure that you are travelling in the right direction. The New Testament makes clear the secret of a successful pilgrimage. You must keep "looking unto Jesus, the author and finisher of our faith".

From the beginning of the Bible to its end, the recurring themes are change and growth. Genesis begins with the image of the spirit of God moving on the face of the waters, bringing order out of chaos. Revelation declares the God who "makes all things new".

It does not ultimately matter whether the great themes of redemption and renewal are expounded in profound theological language or as the simple faith of the one who "takes Jesus at his word". Real living (which the New Testament calls "life abundant") begins with change and issues in growth. The process is dramatically portrayed in the Damascus Road experience of Paul which pointed the former persecutor of Christians, Saul of Tarsus, in an entirely new direction. From then on, his aim was spiritual maturity.

In the kind of world we face today, where materialism and secularism abound, we need to keep to the way of life, focus on the great landmarks of the faith, build a sound theological structure and evolve a philosophy of life that will replace alienation with relationship, meaninglessness with purpose, lostness with rediscovery, fear with love, death with life.

The Garden of the Resurrection demonstrates how death becomes life when you look in a different direction.* Mary, loving her Lord, stood there gazing disconsolately at the place of death. A voice behind her made her turn round. It was the risen Christ. She was no longer looking at death but at life, for she was now looking in the right direction.

* Referred to also in *The Power of Prayer*, Number 18

The Road to Growth

The statement in the letter to the Hebrews in the New Testament which says: "Jesus, the Son of God ... was tempted like as we are," is very important. Theologically, it underlines the truth that he is truly and fully human. Psychologically and spiritually, it brings great comfort. The Master, like the disciples, experiences severe temptation. We can then be assured of the divine understanding of our human failures or, as one comedienne might have put it: "He knows, you know".

While the experience of temptation is common to us all, the focus of it will vary from person to person. Human susceptibility in matters of "the flesh" is, for example, a common failing, but for Jesus it was something different. His three temptations, as recorded by both Matthew and Luke, all relate to that which was unique to him, his awareness of his divine power and gifts. Was he willing to forward his purpose by winning followers through turning stones to bread; creating publicity for himself by leaping from the temple only to land, miraculously, unharmed; engaging in worldly empire-building?

Those subtle inner pressures, tempting him to abuse his power, were firmly resisted and finally rejected. Of the reality of his experience of temptation there is no doubt. That enables him the more to be "God-with-us".

There are two insights in the story of Jesus's temptations that can help us with the pain of spiritual growth. First, it is important to be aware that severe temptation may follow times of spiritual elation. Matthew seems to be suggesting this by his placing the story of Jesus's temptation so close to his greatest spiritual experience, namely the affirmation at his baptism in Jordan: "This is my beloved Son in whom I am well pleased". It is immediately after the recording of this high point, spiritually, that the retailing of the temptation story comes. The closer people get to God the more urgent is it (to personalise the matter) for Satan to step up the attack.

Second, Luke makes a note not recorded in Matthew, but it is a significant one. "When the devil had ended all the temptation, he departed from (Jesus) *for a season*". To this the spiritual struggle in Gethsemane and on the cross surely testifies. It is realistic to recognise as a fact of spiritual life that future failure is always potentially present in us. The graph of the painful journey to spiritual growth is not symbolised by a simple straight line, going onward, rising upward. It is a jagged picture of heights and depths, hills and valleys, peaks and pits, spiritual elation and abject failure. But there is no need to be discouraged. Jesus is "God-with-us", forgiveness is assured and new life promised.

Spiritual Risks

I am a great believer in creative irresponsibility, by which I mean the readiness to fulfil some project likely to be deemed unachievable by 99 out of 100 people, but which the inner spirit says must be undertaken. If such a task is successful, something very creative will have been accomplished. I would not, of course, for one moment defend sheer irresponsibility. On the other hand, being responsible, while laudable, can often be boring and limiting. Creative irresponsibility springs from the sense of adventure which lies between prosaic responsibility and indefensible irresponsibility. I know from experience how creative the products of that attitude can be. The action of Abraham in obediently going out "not knowing whither he went" is a fine biblical example of such valuable irresponsibility. To responsible planners (and even Jesus had a word about the need for planning resources before you set out on a construction project — see Luke 14:28), Abraham's decision to take himself and his extended family on a journey into the unknown must seem utterly irresponsible. In the human perspective it was. In the divine perspective, however, everything is different. Abraham's action carried out in faith and obedience, was divinely creative for the history of Israel and, indeed, for Christian history.

There is something of the feeling of assumed irresponsibility in Paul's recognition of himself and other follows as "fools for Christ's sake". Who, in their senses, would choose to be weak, "a public spectacle", insulted, persecuted, hungry and thirsty, "ill-clad and homeless vagrants," for the sake of religion?* But Paul, and many since him, have found that the irresponsibility of "giving without counting the cost" for the sake of such a cause leads to the wonder of spiritual growth.

Adventurousness involves risk-taking, and that is at the heart of creative irresponsibility. Living in a world that brings about constant tension, unremitting pressure, overwhelming suffering — mass and personal — nervous illness on a huge scale, personal disasters and human tragedies, it is all too easy to drift into negative attitudes to life — defeatism, resentment, envy, jealousy, self-pity.

Our faith, with divine help and human support, must work hard to recapture the sense of adventure inherent in discipleship. The spiritual journey, with its risks and its adventures, may be deemed irresponsible from a human point of view, but those who are "on the way" know they are moving towards "new creation".

* From William Barclay's translation of *I Corinthians, chapter 4, verse 10*

Divine Arithmetic

Multiplication is an important factor in the divine arithmetic. The spiritual law to which it relates is perhaps seen at its simplest in Jesus' statement that "where two or three are gathered together in my name, there am I in the midst of them". There is something about community that increases spiritual energy.

The Christian faith is, on one hand, a highly individualistic religion in that the ultimate questions it poses must be resolved in a one-to-one encounter with God. On the other hand, as I mentioned earlier,* there is a considerable emphasis on fellowship and community in Christianity. It is indeed a corporate religion. Both elements in that paradoxical relationship merit our reflection.

"Whom do you say that I am?" It is the question addressed to the disciples which produces Peter's personal confession. It is the question which confronts each one of us and no one else can answer it for us. When God asks for someone to speak to the people on His behalf, Isaiah answers: "Here am *I, send me*". Doubting Thomas's response to Jesus, who had proved the reality of his resurrection, was intensely personal: "*My* Lord and *my* God". The question put to Jesus by the rich young ruler was equally personal: "What must *I* do to inherit eternal life?" The response was addressed to that individual: "Sell all that *you* have and give it to the poor and ... come, follow *me*." God deals with us individually in matters of salvation. We alone are responsible for our reaction to the offer of grace.

In religion, however, as in life, as John Donne tells us, "no man is an island". Nor is a woman. The vocabulary of the faith is therefore sprinkled with words and concepts that establish its corporate nature — *koinonia* or fellowship, church and community, congregation and flock, the body and its parts, the *people* of God. Of course it is possible to worship God "on the hills" in solitude, but that is a limited discipleship. Response to the miracle of grace involves a commitment to become part of the worshipping, believing fellowship which is committed to the expansion of the kingdom and to serving the world. Robert Herrick in describing Lent underlines our true responsibility. He sees it as a positive giving rather than a negative concern with self:

> *Is it to fast an hour*
> *Or ragg'd to go*
> *Or show*
> *A downcast look and sour?*
> *No: 'tis a fast*
> *To dole thy sheaf of wheat*
> *And meat*
> *Unto the hungry soul*

It is part of the spiritual law of multiplication to understand that while (according to James) "the effectual fervent prayer of a righteous man availeth much", there is a yet greater power in the prayers of a group, two or three — or more — gathered in Christ's name. For in the divine arithmetic, the power of the prayers of a group, meeting with one accord, is far greater than that of its individual members each on their own.

* In *Absolute Demand*, Number 16

The Adventurous Spirit

The Christian faith is an adventure. It involves taking risks. With the quiet mind* and the loving heart** there goes the adventurous spirit. There was a time when his disbelieving disciples were asked by Jesus to "launch out into the deep," there to make their catch. They had just completed a wholly unsuccessful fishing trip, toiling all night and taking nothing. Against their professional judgements, but out of respect for their Lord, they obeyed, launching out in faith. The size of the catch they brought in staggered them.

Abraham had to be obedient to God. He was willing to go wherever God sent him.*** The risks for himself and his family were considerable, but "he went out, not knowing whither he went". It was a total act of faith. In human terms, the adventure made no sense at all, but Abraham would, in due time, see where it was to lead in God's purpose for the children of Israel. Beyond that, it would lead on to God's saving acts for all people in the Incarnation. Only a man of faith could take such risks. His was indeed the adventurous spirit.

Christopher Logue has described the fear of those who were invited to "come to the edge". "It's too high," they said; "We might fall," they cried. But when the invitation was repeated a third time, there was a surprising and thrilling consequence. In response, they *did* come to that edge and take off. *They flew!*

Christianity involves risk. True loving involves risk. But the God who himself dared to "send his Son into the world" to live among us, was taking the risks of love. He expects his followers to demonstrate the adventurous spirit, too.

Paul told the Corinthians that they must be "fools for Christ's sake". This does not mean being irresponsible — that is indefensible — but sometimes a sense of responsibility is just not enough. Between sheer irresponsibility and safe responsibility there is a the "creative irresponsibility" I have already described.**** It is the taking on in faith of tasks that most would dismiss as impossible. It is just there that the adventurous spirit is at work. It is risk-taking for God. But what great things are achieved by those who, in obedience and faith, commit themselves to the adventurous spirit.

* See *The Quiet Mind*, Number 87

** See *The Loving Heart*, Number 31

*** Also referred to in *Spiritual Risks*, Number 28

**** Ibid

Number 31

The Loving Heart

Love is the heartbeat of God. Those who seek to be true to their faith must show the world the loving heart.

The New Testament proclaims the primacy of love. "Love is of God," it says, because "God is love". Jesus himself emphasises the centrality of love by pointing to the two great Old Testament commandments. You must love the Lord your God with your whole being, "heart, soul, mind and strength", *and* your neighbour "as yourself," he says, because "there is no commandment greater than these". Paul adds his word: "Three things last forever — faith, hope, love. But the greatest of these is love".

Is this simply pious God-talk? An escape from reality? The real world is in the news each day — war, violence, prejudice, persecution, pain, suffering, death. Unloving actions, insensitivity to people and needs, the rape of the earth — the news bulletins are full of these unhappy things. So away with spiritual fiction! Come down to earth!

This is exactly what the Bible does! It talks of one who "came down to earth" to be "God with us". "God so loved the world that he gave ..." This is the loving heart of God in action. The disciple has no choice. He or she must be as the Master and offer the world the loving heart.

Our admiration for the saints who have shown us the loving heart in action is boundless — Mother Teresa ministering to the poor, the sick, the dying; Alida Bosshardt of The Salvation Army, exercising her extraordinary ministry in the Red Light district of Amsterdam.* But the loving heart is offered secretly and anonymously too — the devout and devoted nun who spends the whole of her life with the destitute, the devastated and the dying; the priest whose ministry is to "reach out" to the lonely, the despised, the rejected of society, in the pubs and clubs of the teeming city, especially offering a ministry to those who are HIV positive; the hospice carers whose loving hearts help people to cope creatively with death and find healing through dying.

The loving heart is, however, not demanded only from others. It is asked of us all. Like the quiet mind, it is a gift of grace. May the God of Love continually create a multitude of loving hearts.

* See also *Towards the Light*, Number 90

Wine into Water

It was unusual for water to be turned into wine as happened in Jesus's miracle at the wedding in Cana of Galilee. It is all too commonplace in our world today for wine to be turned into water. Trivialisation too often typifies our contemporary culture.

Awe and wonder in the presence of holiness lie at the heart of true religion as great Old Testament characters such as Moses and Isaiah understood so clearly. Moses's face "shone" when he descended from Mount Sinai where he had "talked with God". Isaiah was moved to profound confession for himself and his people when his "eyes had seen the King, the Lord of hosts". The New Testament reflects the same sense of mystery and wonder. Peter, asked who Jesus was, is moved to cry: "Thou art the Christ". Thomas, his doubt defeated, declares: "My Lord and my God". Paul, "caught up to the third heaven ... heard unspeakable words". Mary Magdalene's response to the risen Christ was a devout "Master". No wonder adoration undergirds all Christian worship.

It is the church's responsibility to stimulate the sense of the spiritual and nourish our awareness of the grandeur of God. Paradoxically, the greater the sense of divine love, the deeper the involvement of God's servants in the problems of people.

Wonder, love and praise are not escapist emotions. They are the ground from which compassion comes. The glorification of the trivial endangers the centrality of that which is inherently important. "Behold, they have taken away my Lord, and I know not where they have laid him," says a broken-hearted Mary Magdalene, seeking the crucified Jesus. What she says literally has profound symbolic importance. We can "lose" the Lord in ecclesiastical organisation, institutional minutiae or a super-abundance of activities. The letter of dogmatic theology can obscure the spirit of love and compassion. Yet the priorities of the Christian community do not change. They are proclamation, fellowship and service. The prime task of the church is to be a healing community. Where pride of place is given to activities not closely related to mission and evangelism, the church's work is in danger of trivialisation.

"Your God is too small," wrote J B Phillips. If the grandeur of God is diminished; if limits are set to His all-embracing love; if the sense of the numinous ceases to enliven the human heart; if the Lordship of Christ is taken to the circumference of faith, we are in danger of that trivialisation so typical of sport, entertainment, the media and politics in the ill-balanced life of the world today, often represented by a sensationalism that destroys people and is contrary to love. For, says Paul, "love finds nothing to be glad about when someone goes wrong, but is glad when truth is glad".*

* William Barclay's translation of *I Corinthians, chapter 13, verse 6*

PART II

THE MYSTERY OF
SUFFERING

Divine Compassion

It is such a relief to know that Jesus wept. "Very God of Very God" he may be, as the Nicene creed affirms. Classical Christology may theologise about the two-natures doctrine: "One person in whom are united two natures, a divine and a human, without confusion or change, without division or separation". What the shortest verse in the Bible, "Jesus wept", tells us is that he who was called Son of God is really and truly human. Led there by Mary, like her Jewish companions weeping over their bereavement, Jesus looked into Lazarus's grave and he cried. He was bereaved just as they were and he felt it deeply. He was indeed human. How close, however, are joy and sorrow. "The selfsame well from which your laughter rises was oftentimes filled with your tears," says The Prophet, Kahlil Gibran.* "Joy and sorrow are inseparable. Together they come ... " It was the tears of Mary that took Jesus to the tomb — and to resurrection joy.

Joy and suffering are together at other times in the life of Jesus and his disciples. With whom did he choose to share his glorious Transfiguration experience when the disciples saw him embraced in the light of his future glory? It was Peter, James and John. Who were the disciples he invited to be with him in the place of agonising pain, the Garden of Gethsemane? The same Peter, James and John. Those who shared the wonder of his Transfiguration would share the pain of his Gethsemane.

It was for personal support, surely, that he took them to the Garden, but it was comfort they could not give. Three times he came to awaken them, heavy with sleep. "Could you not watch with me one hour?" he asked. He had had to face the mental and spiritual agony of reaching what William Barclay calls "the point of no return" utterly alone.

That loneliness brings us back to the evidence for Jesus's

true human-ness. He was "panic-stricken" writes Harry Williams,** basing that adjective on Mark's record of the event. "The increasing realisation of what lay ahead came to him with such a sense of overwhelming shock that he was distraught in mind" (Mark, chapter 14, verse 33, William Barclay's translation). "All things are possible with you," he prays. "Take away this cup from me." What human yearning is in that prayer! But obedience, trust and love flow back! "Nevertheless not what I will, but what Thou wilt."

No suffering of ours can equal his, but when we too reach our point of no return, his understanding, sympathy and empathy are guaranteed. He has been there. He knows.

In every human need, the divine compassion is present to share our sadness and our gladness. He wept when Lazarus died. He surely weeps for you in your sorrow. As he shed tears for Jerusalem so, though the reasons are different, he surely weeps for Sarajevo. Because of his Gethsemane, he surely shares our little Gethsemanes. In every sorrow, and joy, he remains Emmanuel — God with us.

* Published by Heinemann
** In *The True Wilderness* (Constable, 1965)

A Time for Tears

If Jesus came to Sarajevo, he would weep. Were he to go to Mogadishu, the tears would roll again. For "Jesus wept" when he learnt that his friend Lazarus was dead. Bereavement made it a time for tears.

There was another occasion when Jesus wept. It was when he came near to Jerusalem that, looking down on the holy city, he felt an overwhelming sense of tragedy. "If only ...," he cried. But he knew what surely must happen: "The time will come when your enemies ... will attack you ... They will level the city to the ground, and you and your children in it. They will not leave one stone standing on another."* It was indeed a time for tears.

It is important to know that Jesus wept. The verse may be the shortest in the Bible, but it is a profound theological statement, for it tells us of the humanity of God. If Jesus is, as the Nicene creed says, "God of God," then we can see in the way that Jesus responds to both people and situations, the way God Himself reacts. It is therefore with confidence that we can say, for our comfort and using human terms, that God's heart bleeds whenever His children suffer. Be it then the death of a friend, the destruction of a city, the death of children on a ferry, the murder of a young mother in Wimbledon, bombs in Belfast, or starvation in Somalia, we can be sure that God feels the pain of His people.

Academic analysis of "the problem of suffering" is fraught with danger. It can so easily lead to the promulgation of pious platitudes that are totally irrelevant at a time when people are shattered by tragedy. Of course it is possible with hindsight to see how God can bring blessing out of hurt and so to believe sincerely that "all things work together for good to them that love God". That is, however, the result of experience over a long time. It is not a text for the day for distraught parents and grieving families. In the hour of desolation it is not words, however well-intentioned, that minister to grief. It is all-embracing love.

The "problem of suffering" remains the greatest of all human issues, and there is much to say on that question. In this world of ever-present and overwhelming suffering, however, the appropriate reaction is not analysis but tears. That is why "Jesus wept".

* Luke, chapter 19, verses 41-44, in William Barclay's translation

By Invitation

It might well have been battered Job who said it, but it was in fact Jacob. Contemplating one loss after another, he uttered his heart-rending cry: "Joseph is not, and Simeon is not; and you will take Benjamin away: *all these things are against me*".

It hurt then, as it hurts today. We all know people who are dogged by disaster, suffer seemingly endless bereavements, wrestle with increasingly complicated illnesses, face one tragedy after another. Out there in the great world, too, there is an ever-increasing mass of anonymous and distressed human beings, victims of war, violence, rape, murder, fire, flood and hunger. It hurts ... wherever it happens, whenever it happens. Is it just bad luck, unhappy coincidence, human circumstance? Or might it be, as in desolation it can feel to be, that God has turned his back and what we are experiencing is judgement?

It is not too difficult to sense the prophet Elijah's desperation, the feeling that he has been left to fight the prophets of Baal alone. "I've had enough," he cries to a seemingly indifferent God. "Lord, take away my life." There are times when the broken heart just has to confess: "I cannot go on!".

Jesus's disciples, caught in a storm on the Sea of Galilee,* had not reached that depth of desolation, but they were out there in the darkness in a tempest and very afraid. It was the fourth watch, around or a little later than 3am,* that time when energy — physical, mental and emotional — is at its lowest, a time when perspective is distorted, when mental turmoil ranges restlessly over insoluble problems. It is not a time to make decisions.

In that darkest hour, Mark tells us, "the winds were contrary" and the disciples were "toiling in rowing". Spiritually too, they were confused. They thought Jesus was a ghost. Mark even comments that "their heart was hardened". They had just seen the miracle of the feeding of the five thousand but, "dully uncomprehending" (William Barclay's translation), they doubted still the wonder of their leader's powers. What they did learn was that it is in the dark, fraught, fearful moments that the presence of Jesus can become dramatically real.

The story of "doubting Thomas" declares the same spiritual truth. "Jesus came, the doors being shut," John tells us. There are many who will testify that it was when in a personal crisis, with every option closed, they sensed the divine presence in their darkness in a most extraordinary way. This is no mere platitude. It is, in fact, a declaration of the doctrine of the Incarnation which means that God is "with us", seeking the lost, healing the broken-hearted and, in the words of Howard Thurman, "making music in the heart".

The story of Jesus's walking on the water also throws into relief a principle witnessed to by his actions on other occasions. As Jesus strode across the water towards the boat, he *"would have passed by them"*. This immediately recalls the story of the walk to Emmaus when "the Stranger", evening drawing nigh, nevertheless *"made as if he would have gone further"*. The message is clear. Jesus comes to needy people only by invitation. The disciples "willingly received him into the ship". The followers on the Emmaus road "constrained" him and pressed him to stay with them — and experienced a miracle.

It is not the divine way to bludgeon anyone into the kingdom of heaven. When the rich young ruler cannot meet the demands of discipleship, Jesus loves him but lets him go. Grace is a gift, always on offer. It must be graciously received.

* See also the reference in *Little Miracles*, Number 10

Amazing Grace

St Paul's Grotto and the catacombs of Rabat, close by the walled city of Mdina in Malta, are present-day reminders of his unscheduled visit to the island. He and his companions were on their way to Rome when they were shipwrecked. The disaster, in providential hands, brought blessings. The winter sojourn of three months affected Malta profoundly. It also provided a specific healing miracle for Publius, the chief magistrate. The curing of his father's dysentery made such an impression that others, too, came for the laying on of hands and — the doctor-reporter Luke records — were healed. When the party could at last leave, he also comments that "they heaped honours upon us". Had the shipwreck not taken place, Malta would have missed an experience.

"I have learned," Paul wrote to the Philippians, "in whatever state I am, therewith to be content" or, as William Barclay expresses it, "I have learned the secret of how to live in any situation and in all circumstances".* That secret Paul surely applied in Malta! When I visited the grotto, I wondered how he and his friends had coped with the claustrophobic conditions in that confined area. But Paul's belief in a Providence that brings the best out of the worst enabled him to effect a miracle of transformation. He made that prison-like abode (there is evidence on its ceiling that it had been used for that purpose) into a place of prayer. A bleak cave was now a chapel. What felt like a cell had become a sanctuary.

When the risen Jesus promised his disciples that they "would receive power after that the Holy Spirit is come upon you", he was pointing to the divine energy that can change both people and situations. It is the "gracious" gift of which John Newton spoke when he wrote of "amazing grace". The divine-human encounter is a healing relationship in which God, in love, takes the initiative. We, graciously receiving, "love him because he first loved us". It is grace that is at the heart of that divine initiative. The aim is our wholeness. Salvation is therefore a gift to be received, not a merit to be earned.

A theology of grace is needed today to prevent our falling victim to the facile optimism that considers human progress inevitable if only we can create the right environment, provide universal education, apply sound psychology, explore new technology. It is a dangerous delusion. These disciplines, each valuable in itself, just cannot reach that deep, dark side of our inner being, corrupted by what both Testaments describe as sin. It is only grace that can deal with our spiritual dilemma, our inability to find God on our own.

"You have made of my life not a tavern, but a temple" wrote the poet** in gratitude for human love. How much greater must be the transformation effected by "the grace that is sufficient". Prisons become sanctuaries. Darkness turns to light. Spiritual death becomes resurrection.

* See also *Creative Discontent*, Number 21
** *I Love You* attributed to Roy Croft

The Pain that Heals

Some 15 years ago, two friends of mine received the dreaded news that they had terminal cancer. One was told she would be able to continue her professional work for a further year at most. For the other, a year was all she could survive. In the same mid-life age-group, both had futures of creative potential, for each had many talents. Suddenly "the future" was limited. They both had appropriate medical treatment, considerable supportive pastoral help within the ministry of healing and much prayer offered on their behalf. The first lady, whom I accompanied to her bank manager so that she could "put her affairs in order", is alive today and fully engaged in her professional work. The second lady, enduring an illness the awfulness of which deeply upset us all, died 15 months after the prognosis had been given. The similarities in many aspects of their stories are remarkable — age-group, diagnosis, treatment — and yet, as the New Testament says in another context, "One was taken and another left". That for me sums up "the mystery of suffering".

The perennially perplexing problem of human suffering feels to have taken on new and frightening dimensions in the cruel world of today. The innocent suffer on a huge scale in the theatres of war and the places of violence; in the destitution of hunger; in the hopelessness of homelessness. Individual suffering is manifest in the spectrum of pain, be it in the physical, emotional, mental or spiritual aspects of being or in all together. With ever greater stridency, the usually plaintive question is voiced: "How can a God of love allow such agonies?". Equally acutely, the question (which all involved in healing ministry must face) illustrated in the stories with which I began, exerts its own pressure. Why is one healed and another not?

The tension between faith and doubt becomes ever more

severe in the face of these familiar but profound ultimate questions. The result of that tension takes those who suffer in two directions. On one hand, there is a steep descent into despondency, depression, anger, resentment and bitterness. On the other, a positive, creative process may just begin to evolve. Whether it is the purpose of suffering (as some would claim) or a by-product of it (as others believe), the experience forces us to look at, test, re-examine our fundamental convictions. Can our simple faith, or (for some) profound intellectual theological structure, cope with the devastating questions thrown up by life? "Lord, I believe," we may cry and, with the father of the sick boy in Mark's Gospel, add "Help thou my unbelief".

One of the most moving statements on the theme of (in the words of the title of one of Dr Martin Israel's books) "the pain that heals" was made to me and a thousand others by a serenely religious woman facing her life crisis. Within the space of a year both she and her husband had been told of their terminal cancers. Facing that situation together, she was able to say with conviction: "We do not know if our cancers have been cured, but we do know that through the experience, we are more whole than we have ever been".

In the midst of the darkness, it is still possible to sense the creative element in suffering. There are those like her who can testify to "the pain that heals".

Healing Words

"Take with you words". The order came from God to the Old Testament prophet, Hosea, as He called him to prayer and penitence. This is a week in which the leaders of nations have turned to words in efforts to prevent wars. The weight of responsibility placed on words has been great indeed.

Stricken, saddened, sorrowing humanity needs healing words. Happily there are words that can relieve the agony of doubt, be the vehicle for profound thoughts, minister to inner distress, bring peace where there is no peace. In the Christian vocabulary there are words of assurance and re-assurance, forgiveness and renewal, acceptance and achievement. On the journey through life we must take with us words of healing.

It is not surprising that, when God chose to come into our world in Jesus Christ, the apostle John welcomed him as "the *Word* made flesh" who "dwelt among us". In that he was moved to compassion by the needs of suffering people, Jesus was "the healing Word" in action. He then sent his disciples out to "preach the Gospel" by proclaiming it in words and to "heal the sick" which was the "acting out" of those words.

Let us, then, reflect on some of the healing words of the New Testament, beginning with "reconciliation" for, as John Milton wrote in Samson Agonistes:

> *Apt words have power to suage*
> *The tumours of a troubled mind*
> *And are as balm to festered wounds.*

The words of Jesus so often brought solace to distressed and despairing people. "Come unto me," he said, "all ye that labour and are heavy-laden, and I will give you rest." "Peace I leave with you," he said, "not as the world giveth give I to you. Let not your heart be troubled, neither let it be afraid."

Let us his followers take with us healing words. Such words can be an instrument of peace, an orchestration of joy, a symphony of the sounds of salvation.

Reconciliation

Reconciliation is a healing word. It has nothing to do with softness or appeasement. It refers to determined and costly effort to mend broken relationships. The Christian symbol, the cross, declares the cost of God's reconciling act in Jesus Christ. The Christian is, consequently, committed to the ministry of reconciliation.

In a war-torn world, bleeding to death because of broken relationships at so many levels, there is an obligation on us all to "take with us" the healing word, reconciliation, wherever we go. Across the divisions that fragment the world and violate the essential "one-ness" of humanity, the Bible exhorts us to be reconciled to one another.

When Paul speaks of reconciliation, he never talks of human beings reconciling men and women to God. He does speak of "God reconciling man to himself". In other words, as the late Professor William Barclay reminds us: "It was not God who needed to be pacified, but man who needed to be moved to surrender, penitence and love".

If this religious language feels foreign to the world of today, we can express it in contemporary terms. "Lostness", "alienation" and "meaninglessness" are very much part of our present experience. Negative feelings of that kind dominate the lives of many who find their way to psychiatric hospitals, psychotherapeutic agencies and counselling centres. Many more try to cope with such stressful feelings on their own. Alienation is the experience of being (metaphorically) a stranger in a foreign land, cut off from one's roots and out of relationships with people. It leaves life lacking in meaning and purpose.

But that is precisely the parable of the prodigal son in modern terms. It is a story that Jesus told about lostness ("for this my son was lost"), alienation ("in a far country") and meaninglessness (sharing with pigs while, at home, the board is spread). It is a parable about reconciliation — a waiting father, who is not there to rebuke, but to receive. It was not the father who "needed to be pacified". It was the son who was "moved to penitence and love". Significantly there follows a ministry of reconciliation towards the resentful elder brother. This is the way God acts, Jesus is telling us. He restores relationships. He effects reconciliation.

Take with you into this shattered world, the word of reconciliation. It is the healing word brought to us by and in Jesus.

Acceptance

Acceptance is a contemporary word. It occurs once in the Bible, but it is used there in another sense. "Being accepted" reflects a particular experience, well understood by most people today. That experience is wholly biblical. Acceptance, then, is one of the healing words needed by the world. Accepting love is the Gospel in action.

We have reflected on the healing word "reconciliation" and in doing so thought about the parable of the prodigal son. Recall again that image of the father as he runs, arms outstretched in potential embrace, to meet his lost son. That image incarnates the words "accepting love". No criticism, rebuke or condemnation (which he expected) met that son. What he unexpectedly received was unconditional acceptance. That element of unexpectedness characterises the biblical understanding of acceptance.

Consider the story of "the woman taken in adultery" (John, chapter 8, verses 1-11). This story has been questioned as to its authenticity because it is not in some important manuscripts, but it has (in J B Phillips' phrase) "a ring of truth" about it. The woman was taken to Jesus by her accusers, the scribes and Pharisees. They reminded Jesus that the punishment laid down in the law of Moses for adultery was stoning. Then the unexpected happened. Jesus suggested that anyone who was without sin should administer the punishment. One by one her accusers slipped away in total discomfort. The woman, however, received accepting love from Jesus who did not condone her sin (he told her not to do it again) but offered her no condemnation. The unexpectedness of his acceptance of her must have touched her deeply.

Then there was "the woman of bad reputation" who, in the house of Simon the Pharisee, washed the feet of Jesus with her tears and wiped them dry with her hair (Luke, chapter 7, verses 36-50). Again the tables are turned by Jesus's accepting love. The technically religious Simon is "told off".* The woman who was technically a sinner was, with her sincere and genuine love, totally accepted.

If the receiving of mercy compels us to show mercy — as it does; if being forgiven commits us to forgive others — as it does; if we find ourselves the recipients of the accepting love of God — which we do; we are bound to offer acceptance to others, whatever their situation.

Acceptance is indeed a healing word.

* See also *Acts of Love*, Number 61

A Sense of Distance

There are two more healing words to "take with us". One is, not surprisingly, closeness. The other, perhaps surprisingly, is distance. Both are strikingly illustrated in Jesus's ministry.

John tells us in his Gospel that "Jesus knew what was in man" ... and woman. It was his "divine intuition" which enabled him to enter into relationships with all kinds of people ... like Nicodemus, who came to him secretly, by night; the woman from Samaria, whom he met at the well of Sychar; Zacchaeus, the despised tax gatherer; the woman "taken in adultery" by her self-righteous accusers. Jesus exercised his "ministry of closeness" to each one in whatever form they needed it and to whatever degree was appropriate. He gave people trust and, as a result, a sense of value. The followers of Jesus must reflect Jesus's sensitivity as they offer *their* ministry of closeness and, in so doing, help people to feel better.

There are times, however, when people need not closeness, but distance. The ministry of distance also requires great sensitivity. There is the Gospel story of the rich young ruler who could not meet the demands of discipleship because "he had great possessions". Jesus respected his decision. Looking at the young man as he slipped sorrowfully away, Jesus "loved him" - and let him go. He needed distance.

The prodigal son needed space to help him find right relationships. He went to "a far country" and, from that distance, learnt what home and values meant.

When his friend Lazarus died, Jesus stayed away from Bethany for two days. It seems extraordinary that, loving Lazarus's sisters Martha and Mary as he did, Jesus should deliberately remain at a distance from them, but the ministry of distance would contribute to the miracle of Lazarus's resurrection. There are times when closeness is inappropriate and distance is in the interests of all.

We return to the concept of closeness in order to note finally that Jesus often expressed that ministry by touch. He laid hands on the sick and the blind. He touched the leper. He took the children in his arms, laid his hands on them and blessed them. In return there were those who wanted to touch him ... the woman who struggled to touch "the hem of his garment", Mary reaching out to touch him in the Garden of the Resurrection.

Touch, too, is a healing word.*

* See the development of this theme in *The Ministry of Touch*, Number 71

Healing through Suffering

Each of our lives has its quota of suffering. Does the Psalmist really mean what he says, namely that suffering is good for you? "It is good for me that I have been afflicted that I might learn thy statutes" (Psalm 119, verse 71).

The result of such a platitude, often pronounced by preachers not suffering greatly, can only be anger, resentment and rebellion. In any congregation there may well be the terminally ill, the HIV sufferer, the relations of someone suffering from Alzheimer's Disease. Such negative reactions are understandable. But we must consider the concept of "healing through suffering" and look in two directions for help in doing so.

First, we go to the Bible. What the Psalmist said was that *with hindsight* he sees that he has learnt much through his "affliction". Paul, too, talks of "present suffering and future glory", while Jesus says something similar: "In the world you shall have tribulation, but be of good cheer, I have overcome the world". The Bible does seem to say that out of present pain there can come future blessing.

The ultimate authority is, secondly, the testimony of those who actually suffer greatly — like Lin Berwick.* Cerebral-palsied from birth, in a wheelchair for life, blind since her teens, Lin trained as a counsellor, works in the bereavement field, counsels the disabled in sexual problems, was a counsellor on a television programme and to a disability newspaper. An accredited Methodist preacher, she speaks from her wheelchair. She also lectures, has written her life story and has set up a trust to provide holiday accommodation for disabled people. She knows she has grown greatly through her pain. "*The best things I have done for God, I have done since I became blind*," she says. God does not "send" suffering, but when it comes He is present to lead the sufferer, if the response is not bitterness but positive acceptance, towards wholeness.

Whatever suffering or pain comes, be it personal or corporate, may we receive the grace to grow through it. This is part of the ministry of healing.

Coping with Anxiety

One of the privileges of pastoral ministry is close contact with the "aged saints", those who, far advanced in years, are physically so weak, yet spiritually so strong. In their "closer walk with God", they have gained deep insights into human need and divine grace. But one thing concerns many of them. Their helplessness means they can *do* nothing to ease the world's pain. But they can and do pray fervently. I always suggest that they should bless the world by praying for "the healing of the atmosphere".

"Doom and gloom" is a phrase constantly used today as economic, social and international problems escalate; as the financial constraints bring worry to individuals and businesses; as many struggle to keep homes and families together. An infectious despair pervades large areas of society. With so much that is negative seeping into the atmosphere, we are becoming an increasingly unhealthy people, with widespread stress, nervous illnesses, debilitating depression, individual and corporate anxiety abounding.

The great Methodist preacher, Leslie Weatherhead, coined a phrase for his time and many years ago made it the title of one of his numerous books. What he offered, through uniting the insights of psychology with the truths of religion, was a "prescription for anxiety".* That it was a relevant prescription for many human needs was demonstrated by the numbers who came to hear him preach; at the same time he offered them a psychotherapeutic, analytic approach to healing. It is even more relevant today.

The pain of facing the inner, unconscious world from which so many of our "problems" come is, although invaluable for some, difficult for many. It is, however, possible to offer, even if it is in a much simpler, more limited way, a charter of encouragement to creative attitudes. It comes from Paul's first letter to the Thessalonian community, and offers five positive principles:

- **Rejoice evermore:** the Christian theme is resurrection and therefore victory. A theology of joy is an antidote to doom and gloom.

- **Pray without ceasing:** this is not an instruction to pray without stopping. It is a reminder that prayer is a way of life, that which maintains and develops relationship with Christ. The fruits of such a relationship can only be creative.

- **In everything, give thanks**: a grateful heart is life-enhancing.

- **See that none renders evil for evil:** revenge is negative and destructive. Reconciliation is positive and creative.

- **Quench not the Spirit:** how sad it is that so often, even within the religious community, spontaneity is discouraged, enthusiasm dampened, initiative discounted, change consistently opposed. How much more is *enthusiasm* a mark of the Spirit's presence, for "enthusiasm" is a word with God (*theos*) at its heart.

Joy, prayer, gratitude, reconciliation and enthusiasm — these attitudes by themselves cannot deal with the deep roots of anxiety, but they may offer some kind of simple prescription for a more creative life.

---

* *Prescription for Anxiety* (Arthur James)

No Easy Way

"Prophecy, excellent! Impact, nil!" That was the damning divine report on the prophet Ezekiel's attempts to convey to God's people His word for today (Ezekiel, chapter 33, verses 30-32). The report is worth quoting.*

> *The people say: "Let's go and hear what word has come from the Lord now." So my people crowd in to hear what you have to say, but they don't do what you tell them to do. Loving words are on their lips, but they continue their greedy ways. To them you are nothing more than an entertainer singing love-songs or playing a harp. They listen to all your words and don't obey a single one of them.*

What a fascinating cameo! It throws into relief so dramatically a perennial problem of the faith — that of successful communication. How do you proclaim effectively *the unchanging Word to a rapidly changing world*? Yet the Bible remains contemporary, the teaching of Jesus is respected far outside the circle of his followers, the great verities of the faith — incarnation, resurrection, the coming of the Spirit — continue to be the only ultimate answers to the human dilemma.

The problem is compounded by the generation gap — in lifestyles, attitudes, understanding. When I need help with any item of communication technology, I go to my grandson, for what is a mystery to me is child's play to him! Humbly I realise the differences that characterise the generations. Yet it is to such disparate groups, with all their infinite variations in standpoints and styles, that the unchanging Word has to be proclaimed.

Consider these two matters, related to this theme. The first concerns inner authority. This Jesus had. Indeed the people were "astonished ... for he taught them as one having authority, and not as the scribes". Successful communication depends on real inner authority.

The second issue asks the question: which is more likely to attract the seeker — a faith which accommodates its standards to make them less demanding, or one that tells its disciples there is no easy way to spiritual maturity? The facts provide the answer. The growing churches are those which demand profound commitment, continuing prayer and consecrated service. A faith which makes it too easy is a faith no one wants.

* *The Good News Bible* (HarperCollins)

Right Relationships

How sad it is when loving relationships break down. In that "love finds nothing to be glad about when someone goes wrong, but is glad when truth is glad",* dramatising others' pain for satisfaction or profit is unacceptable. The reality is that love and relationship are both essential to human well-being. The primacy of love is written large in the Old Testament. To love God and our neighbour is the first and great commandment, says the New Testament. We shall come as close to inner health and spiritual wholeness as possible when all our relationships are in good order ... our relationship upward to God, downward to the earth, outward to others and inward to ourselves.

The Earth Summit has reminded us of the need for a positive, creative relationship to the ground. "The earth is the Lord's", proclaims the Psalmist. The Incarnation has demonstrated God's sharing in the life of the world, for it was on our earth that Jesus walked, preached and healed. The Creator committed His world into human hands and sought to be glorified through their stewardship of its resources. Human beings cannot therefore stand aside unaffected while the earth is abused, the atmosphere polluted, the living world destroyed. Our corporate failure in stewardship has damaged God's world and is destroying His creatures. How right it is that we are being compelled to re-assess our relationship to the earth.

If broken personal relationships are indeed hurtful, how increasingly awful are the consequences of fractured relationships in our national and international life? Look where you will in the world — here, where good men die on public duty; or in the world's troubled places where the innocent victims of wars, violence, aggression, racial prejudice, starvation (whether brought about by drought, aggression or selfish economics), the dominating word is division, the missing word, reconciliation. Yet the biblical message is clear. You cannot hate your brother or sister and at the same time claim you love God.

The need for a right relationship with ourselves demands courageous self-understanding, especially in the obligation to accept the unacceptable side of our being. If we cannot learn to love our shadow selves, we will never be able fully to love our neighbour.

Loving our world, our neighbour and ourselves can grow only if that fourth, fundamental relationship is sound, our relationship "upward" to God. Loving relationships are founded, fed and forwarded by our love for God and, even more, His love for us.

* William Barclay's translation of I Corinthians, chapter 13, verse 6

Saved by Hope

Sue Barker, tennis player turned television commentator, was interviewed on *Sport on 4* by the Welsh rugby legend, now a radio presenter, Cliff Morgan. Monica Seles had been stabbed on court at a major tournament that week and the conversation turned to the need for security. Finally the unthinkable was mentioned as a future possibility — Wimbledon fenced in. With great feeling and profound sadness, Cliff Morgan said (if I recall his words exactly), "It really is a lousy world in which we are living!".

I hesitate as I quote the word "lousy". When a child, I was taught that it was a word which was not quite "drawing-room". The inhibition remains. But the synonyms I find in my thesaurus — nauseating, sickening, revolting, shocking, detestable, etc — do not as accurately express just what Cliff Morgan felt. Reluctantly but realistically, I accept his word. The world of today feels an increasingly "lousy" world.

A brick was hurled through my car window recently, for no reason but vandalism. It was a symptom of the evil in the world. But that incident, compared with other things, is utterly trivial. Monstrous things are constantly happening today — the murder of children, the mugging of the frail, the violent rape of women, so much spilt blood in Bosnia (and many other places), bereavement in Belfast (and many other places), starvation in the Sudan, terror in Somalia. We can go on and on in this vein as each day brings news of large-scale pain and suffering. Cliff Morgan's plaintive cry reflects the despair now so prevalent in the world. We may even be tempted to cry "Stop the world! I want to get off!".

But people of faith cannot contract out of life, however desperate they feel it to be, for this is the world created by God in love, the world "God so loved that He gave His only-begotten Son" for it. This is the world in which Jesus lived, taught and healed, the world on which he set such a value that he died for it. This is the world in which that "living energy of a loving God", the Holy Spirit, moves and, like the wind, blows where it chooses. The world may, in John Baillie's phrase, be "a good thing spoiled", but it is still God's world; the world with which in forgiveness and redemption He has a relationship of love; the world He longs to change.

The vocabulary of faith is full of words about change — renewal, regeneration, redemption, transformation, sanctification. Fundamental to faith is the conviction that "amazing grace" can bring about change in individuals and, through them, in society. To surrender belief in the possibility of change is to deny the power promised by God to His world.

To succumb to despair is to destroy the future. We are, as the Good Book reminds us, "saved by *hope*".

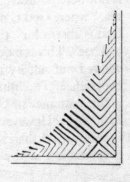

Gentle Sleep

"O sleep! O gentle sleep! Nature's soft nurse ..."* The ability
to fall asleep, and sleep soundly, is a gift for which continual
thanks should be offered. Sadly there are those, perhaps many,
who just cannot sleep well and so have to endure dreaded
"long night watches" with their anxiety and indeed agony.
The middle of the night is, for some, life's lowest point. The
divine Presence can seem far away at 3am.

I remember well the text on which I was asked to preach
in the "sermon class" when I was training for the ministry
in Edinburgh University's Faculty of Divinity. It runs "When
I awake, I am still with thee".

That statement is a glorious affirmation of a doctrine
fundamental to faith, the belief in Providence. We may be
unconscious in sleep but, as the Psalmist explains in
"comfortable words": "Behold, he that keepeth Israel shall
neither slumber nor sleep" (Psalm 121). We are, to put it
in very human terms, in the care of an ever-wakeful and ever-
watchful God, day and, even more importantly, night.

The Psalm from which my sermon class text comes (Psalm
139) describes dramatically the uniquely present Creator and,
in New Testament language, Father. "Whither shall I flee from
Thy presence?" the Psalmist asks. His answer is that there
is nowhere, in heaven or hell, in "the uttermost parts of the
sea", where God is not present. Nor is there any time when
God is absent for "the darkness and the light are both alike
to Thee". This is indeed the Psalmist's doctrine of providence
worked out not by intellectual reasoning but out of living
experience. The important part for those who cannot sleep
is the assurance of God's presence *in the darkness as well as
in daylight*. However hard it is to believe it, and even more
to feel it, God shares our sleepless hell. The divine Presence
is there even, and perhaps especially, at 3am.

It is, alas, much easier to affirm this spiritual truth than to apply it and immediately fall asleep. A night-time of physical, mental, emotional and/or spiritual restlessness takes away our sense of perspective. The worries associated with family, business, unemployment, illness, bereavement draw to themselves an exaggerated unreality. The facts with which we can courageously cope by day become ominously threatening by night. Is there any spiritual resource for this turmoil?

It would be much too facile to suggest that anxious sleeplessness can be spontaneously banished by spiritual reflection, but if the sense of God's providence is an active element in our faith, our spirituality should provide some solace. Recalling some "comfortable words" from the Psalms; repeating over and over again reassuring words from Jesus — "I will not leave you comfortless", "my peace I give to you"; a silent prayer, perhaps to be able to "be still" — all these can be of benefit.

To fall asleep is an act of trust. How blessed are those who can take this step and awake to a lively sense of God's omnipresence. In the receiving of such blessings, remember at the same time those for whom, sadly, there is no gentle sleep.

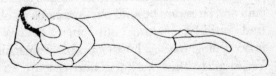

* *William Shakespeare: Henry IV, part 2*

Perchance to dream

"To sleep; to sleep; perchance to dream," mused Hamlet. Dreams certainly feature in the Bible. The dreams in which the Old Testament Joseph became involved as an interpreter had a major prophetic element about them. In the New Testament, Mary's husband Joseph — a man of profound intuition, sensitive spirituality and religious awareness — experienced his dreams as divine warnings. The safety of the infant Jesus depended on his not only listening to his dreams but acting on them, in obedience to the divine will.

Modern psychology uses a different vocabulary in defining dreams. The Jungian therapist Carol Jeffrey (of The Open Way) saw the creative potential in dreams. "A dream," she once said, "is a photograph, *a snapshot of an area of the unconscious*." Studying your dream "will lead to recognition and new perception of aspects, attitudes, functioning and knowledge. Revelation of this kind can provide guidance, wisdom, warning and stimulation, and lead to change and sometimes to the dynamic development of unused potential, hitherto unknown".

The unconscious is perhaps most simply described as a tape-recording of life's total experience from birth, possibly even before it. If our first contacts were warm, welcoming and loving, our emotional security in later life will be the greater. If, however, we suffered rejection and sensed no love, those negative experiences, recorded on life's tape, may well express themselves at some time in unacceptable attitudes and problem behaviour. Because the reasons for our unhappiness, pain and stress are beyond our conscious recollection we may find ourselves acting out our "shadow" feelings in unacceptable ways ... hurting people, damaging relationships. Yet in all truth, "we know not what we do" — nor why.

To fall asleep is an act of trust in which we deliberately lose consciousness but, like the ever-wakeful, ever-watchful God of Psalm 121, our *unconscious* "neither slumbers not sleeps". With our defences down, material from that area may well express itself in dreams. If such material is positive, our creativity will be ultimately enhanced, but when negative material breaks through to give us uneasy feelings, our dreams may become nightmares. And because such "shadow" material *is* threatening, it will be expressed in complex symbolic forms.

In the dark hours of the night, when physical, nervous and spiritual energy is at a low ebb, how frightening our dreams can be! Fear and anxiety may well threaten our inner security while unresolved guilt, especially of an inappropriate kind, can destroy our peace. There is no spiritual magic that can, in the twinkling of an eye, banish those threats but our spirituality, if real, should provide some solace. Outgoing love to others can help to disperse the fear that comes from anxiety about self (for, John tells us, "perfect love casts out fear").

For those struggling with guilt, our spiritual resource is the greatest of the articles of the faith, the doctrine of forgiveness. It is in the assurance of forgiveness as described by Jesus — infinite, repetitive, "full and free" — that the possibility of feeling something of that peace which "passeth understanding" can become authentic. The peace that "the world cannot give or take away" may even begin to be sensed as real in the dark hours of the night, telling us — as the life, death and resurrection of Jesus show — that the darkest hour is just before the dawn.

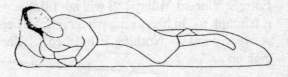

"He is risen!"

"Death is going back-stage to meet the Author." Only someone from the world of entertainment could have said that — and did. The words are Donald Swann's. He died last week.

I knew Donald as a friend of many years and respected him enormously. When, in the sixties, I wanted to explore the possibility of "communication through the arts", it was to Donald, his great friend Sydney Carter, Nadia Cattouse, Sylvia Read and William Fry (Theatre Roundabout) and others that I turned. Donald's contribution was particularly important because he was an explorer of "the things that are eternal", and did just that in his own presentation for us, *Soundings by Swann*. He is remembered, however, mainly as the (Sydney Carter's affectionate word) "hobbit-like" half of that famous partnership, Flanders and Swann. How extraordinarily successful were their shows, *At the Drop of a Hat* and *At the Drop of Another Hat*, with those familiar songs and gently satirical lyrics! I last heard Donald play and sing *Mud, Mud, Glorious Mud* publicly less than a year ago. He was "backed" by a distinguished chorus — Ian Wallace, John Amis, Frank Topping, Sydney Carter and others. How marvellous it was, for he was then very ill! But Donald needs to be remembered for his own serious work in composition, his passion for peace, his sense of the spiritual.

In the Coda which he added to his autobiography *Swann's Way: A Life in Song* (the paperback edition*), Donald writes of the cancer against which he battled so courageously for so long. "Thou famished grave" he quoted defiantly (from Edna St Vincent Millay), "I will not fill thee yet". And there is triumph too in his closing paragraph: "There is continuity at every point ... Nothing is finished ... The stream flows ever on ...".

How fitting it felt to quote these words at Eastertide (he died in March). The disciples too were pointed *forward* by the message from the Garden of the Resurrection: "He is risen: he is not here ... he goeth before you into Galilee". It brings a ring of truth to the assurances from Jesus: "Lo, I am with you always"; "I will not leave you comfortless: I will come to you". And from Paul: "O death, where is thy sting? O grave, where is thy victory? Thanks be to God who giveth us the victory through our Lord Jesus Christ". Nothing, truly, is finished.

The theme of salvation focuses on three gardens. The first is the Garden of Eden, the garden of human failure where, as that profound Genesis story demonstrates, God's gift of freedom was abused in deliberate disobedience to His will. The second is the Garden of Gethsemane where Jesus feared, faced and accepted that he is "the Lamb of God who taketh away the sin of the world". It is in the wonder of the third, the Garden of the Resurrection, that the seal is set on his victory over sin and death. The empty tomb proclaims his resurrection. The stream flows on.

Nothing is finished. The Garden of the Resurrection is not the place of ending, but of beginning.

"He is risen!". Alleluia!

* Published by Arthur James, 1993

The Silence of Dignity

The Christian emphasis on the value of silence is increasingly important in this noisy world. The Psalmist's advice to "be still" is timely. Words are and must be the normal method of communication, but it is right to remember the power of silence to convey great thoughts and to express deep feelings.

Silence is, for example, invaluable in prayer. Only by listening to "the still, small voice" can we discern the will of God. Silence in relation to people is an obligation of Christian love, Paul tells us, for "love finds nothing to be glad about when someone goes wrong, but is glad when truth is glad". Gossip and sensationalism are not part of the loving way.

The silence of awe and wonder, such a natural part of the spirituality of those in Bible days, is largely missing from contemporary attitudes. Many people are no longer even moved by the sheer holiness of God. Even within the church, there is a need to recover "the sense of the numinous". It is however the silence of dignity on which I ask you to reflect in this meditation.

Jesus has been called before his accusers — elders, priests, Herod. Insulting accusations are made against him and blasphemous things said. The Gospels record the situation succinctly. *Jesus answered them nothing*. That silence of dignity was the only appropriate response. It was, at the same time, a most effective contribution. There are some things in life which do not merit serious consideration. There are people to whom nothing relevant can be said. Verbal persecution is not dealt with best by counter-accusation. It is not words but silence that makes the point.

There is within us all a natural desire to offer eye for eye, argument for argument, accusation for accusation. That is understandably human and at times may even be appropriate. There may well arise situations, however, when the right answer is no answer; when strident argument is destructive and negative; when that which is potentially creative lies in "accentuating the positive" aspects of faith. Jesus offers us all the example of an attitude that he was able to show when under great pressure. It is an attitude to life and to people that is not easy to acquire, but it is one that it is indeed desirable to cultivate.

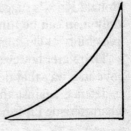

A Time to Laugh

"There is a time to laugh," declares The Preacher (Ecclesiastes) in the Old Testament. To remember the truth of that statement is essential for our health and well-being, physically, psychologically, mentally and, indeed, spiritually.

There is, of course, also "a time to weep"; as we all know, there is much weeping in the world today. Filled as the media is with reports of death and destruction, starvation and disease, doom and gloom, it is essential that, in the interests of balance (a useful synonym for health), we honour, cultivate and demonstrate the capacity to laugh. "Laughter," said Thomas Hobbes in *Human Nature*, "is nothing else than sudden glory."

The evidences of "the fruit of the Spirit" are "love, joy, peace, long-suffering, gentleness, goodness, faith, meekness and temperance".* Discussing these products of "the harvest of the Spirit" in a book that I wrote some years ago,** I ended by suggesting some other qualities that seemed to belong to that harvest. They included compassion, empathy, friendship, the ability to encourage, and a sense of humour. That last one is surely a God-given gift. Religious people, especially those given to over-earnestness, need to discover, sustain and develop their ability to laugh — at themselves, at pomposity, at their less worthy reactions to people, at their mistakes.

Elizabeth Templeton, an outstanding young Scottish theologian, notes in her essay on *The Possibility of Laughter*, Ronald Knox's suggestion that because only man has dignity, only man can be funny. She adds her own comment: "The possibility of laughter belongs intimately to our humanness".

There are, however, those who turn every situation into a joke in a way that destroys serious discussion. That is often a defence against their vulnerability, but it can become a characteristic flippancy which prevents career progress. There is a time to laugh, but it is not all the time.

Just because our world is a vale of tears, there is a responsibility on all who believe in a theology of laughter to ensure that the blessings of humour, happiness and pleasure are available to all. The value of the ability to smile is underlined in Mother Teresa's classic words:

"Let there be kindness in your face, in your eyes and in the warmth of your greeting. For children, for the poor, for all who suffer and are alone, *always have a happy smile*. Give them not only your care, but your heart."

There is a time to smile and a time to laugh.

* For a similar list of the fruits of the Spirit in William Barclay's translation, see *A Positive Faith*, Number 56

** *Love, the Word that heals* (now out of print)

A Sense of Destiny

"Hope is the future tense of faith," writes Bishop Richard Holloway.* It is hope that compels the Christian faith to be forward-looking, conscious of divine purpose, anticipating future glory, encouraging a sense of destiny. We are indeed, as Paul told the Romans, "saved by hope".

That awareness of divine destiny manifested itself frequently in the Bible. "Speak unto the children of Israel that they *go forward*," God tells Moses. It is an invitation to reach out and fulfil their destiny within God's purpose.

Abraham, as we noted earlier,** "went out, not knowing whither he went". This was both an act of obedience and a commitment to destiny in that "he looked for a city which hath foundations whose builder and maker is God".

Paul saw his destiny as the attainment of the spiritual goal. "I press toward the mark for the prize of the high calling of God in Christ Jesus," he told the Philippian church. It is a sense of destiny that helps to create the energy which makes us go on.

We have therefore four elements that provide a secure base from which we can face an unknown future in an uncertain world — a sense of direction, a sense of perspective, a sense of adventure and a sense of destiny. But what of security? Such is the potential violence of our modern world that not a day passes without a mention of that word.

How ironic it is, then, that this same world is psychologically, emotionally and spiritually gravely insecure! The loss of theological and ethical landmarks, the decreasing authority of the Church, the constant erosion of traditional standards and values, the questioning of institutions, the revolution in attitudes to marriage and relationships, the obsession with possessions and gain — all these trends have combined to create in many people those negative characteristics already mentioned, rootlessness, alienation, meaninglessness and lostness. Inevitably, nervous and mental breakdowns abound, while others increasingly find themselves unable to cope with the economic, psychological and social demands of life. It is, sadly, dis-ease rather than health that dominates our times.

It is part of our belief in a loving Providence to feel not only that God is *with* us, but also that He goes *before* us. The Eastern shepherd who leads his sheep to ensure their safety is one biblical model for that truth. Another is the picture of the Israelites on their journey to the promised land as God "went before them by day in a pillar of cloud, to lead them the way".

"We love Him because He *first* loved us," John writes in the New Testament. His, in Emil Brunner's phrase, is "the divine initiative". We have a sense of destiny because we know that He leads the way.

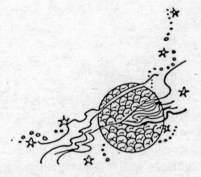

* *Anger, Sex, Doubt and Death* by Richard Holloway, (SPCK 1992)

** See *Spiritual Risks*, Number 28; *The Adventurous Spirit*, Number 30 and *The Loving Heart*, Number 31

PART III

PEOPLE MATTER

People Matter

The life of Jesus demonstrated how to deal with people. At the heart of the Gospel there lies a profound concern for human beings "made in the image of God". With compassion, sensitivity and understanding, Jesus acted out the essence of the message that he brought, namely that "God is love". He therefore made it clear that people matter.

Christianity is about relationship — relationship with God, with others, with the earth and with ourselves. The New Testament offers, in Christ, the opportunity for the restoration of a right relationship with God. If, deep in the Divine heart, there is a yearning for relationship with created beings, it clearly means that people are of infinite importance in the economy of God.

When Paul wrote to the Philippians, he presented Jesus as our model. You must have "the mind of Jesus", he said. He was thinking primarily of the exemplary humility of Christ, but certainly in Professor William Barclay's translation of the New Testament, the advice seems to be widened. He says: "Try to have the same attitude to life that Jesus had". It is Jesus's attitude to life, to human situations and, especially, to people that occupies our attention in these Meditations. He had a unique ability to be at ease with the rich and the poor, the intellectual and the uneducated, male and female, Jew and Samaritan. He brought to people sympathy and empathy, understanding and encouragement, appropriate words and gestures. As he himself said, he "knew what was in man" ... and woman, and child ... and he showed that he did.

It was therefore the sheer quality of his attitudes to life and people that enabled Jesus to offer comfort or criticism; to relate intimately or to know when to keep at a distance; to challenge people to discipleship or to respect the decision of those who could not face his demands. As we look at these incidents we shall see how Jesus showed, by his attitudes, the unique importance of every individual, that indeed people matter.

In a world utterly overwhelmed by mass suffering on an unbelievable scale, it is important that we feel again the Gospel emphasis on the value of each and every human being. It is after all (says Jesus) "not the will of your Father in heaven that *one* of these little ones should perish". Everybody matters.

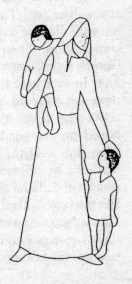

Be Sensitive!

So sensitive was Jesus to the suffering of people that he was constantly "moved to compassion". His was a loving concern for people in need. He expressed that concern in miracles of healing. It was, for example, his awareness of the inner turmoil in Zacchaeus that brought about the healing relationship that transformed the despised tax-gatherer. It was with similar perception that he used his encounters with Nicodemus and "a woman of Samaria" as evangelical opportunities. Jesus showed these two people the deep needs they had, but of which they were unaware. Sensitivity and compassion were essential elements in the attitude to life and people that Jesus had.

Nicodemus visited Jesus secretly, "by night". That a Pharisee, "a master of Israel", should do something so risky testifies to the sincerity of his search for truth. The meeting with the woman of Samaria came about when Jesus was on his way back to Galilee. Going through Samaria, he stopped at a well to rest. The woman arrived to draw water, totally unaware that she was about to be involved in deeply spiritual conversation. These two incidents are recorded in John's Gospel, significantly close to each other in chapters three and four. In each case the conversation seems, at first sight, to represent a failure in communication. To Jesus's statement about the necessity of being spiritually "born again", Nicodemus responds with a question about the possibility of *physical* re-birth. "Can one enter a second time into one's mother's womb and be born?" he asks. Jesus talks to the woman of Samaria about the "living water" which he offers. Her response is to raise the practical problem of drawing water from a deep well without proper equipment. Jesus leads both these conversations into deeply spiritual areas, declaring the essence of the Gospel to Nicodemus and defining the meaning of true worship to the Samaritan woman.

The results of these exercises in evangelism are striking. That same Nicodemus was with Joseph of Arimathea when he asked to be given the body of Jesus after his crucifixion in order to tend it with care. It was the woman of Samaria who testified to her own people: "Is not this the Christ?" It is important that all who are involved in evangelical endeavour today reflect the sensitivity and compassion which Jesus showed to those whom he sought to lead towards the truth.

Love in Action

The attitude to life and people that Jesus had was grounded in the scriptures of the Old Testament. Appointed to read the lesson in his home town synagogue in Nazareth, Jesus found himself saying: "The Spirit of the Lord is upon me, because he hath anointed me to preach the Gospel to the poor; he hath sent me to heal the broken-hearted, to preach deliverance to the captives, and recovering of sight to the blind, to set at liberty them that are bruised, to preach the acceptable year of the Lord".

With a genuine sense of drama, he told the congregation that those very words were being fulfilled that day in him. It is, then, not surprising that when he was ready to "send out" his disciples he should tell them, quite specifically, to "preach the Gospel" *and* "heal the sick".

A large number of healing miracles are recorded in the Gospels. These acts of compassion represent the divine love in action. Preaching the Gospel and healing the sick are, in effect, but two sides of a coin. The latter is the former "acted out".*

Jesus put the greatest possible value on the physical healings that he carried out. As he told John the Baptist, in response to John's message from prison that seemed to question Jesus's Messiahship, miracles (such as those which enabled the blind to see and the deaf to hear) authenticated his divine calling. They witnessed to "the power of the Kingdom" present in him.

But human beings need more than physical cures. They need to be healed emotionally, mentally and spiritually. When a man who was "sick of the palsy" was healed by Jesus he was told: "Arise, take up thy bed and walk!". But, as the spectator scribes confirmed by their questioning of his right to say it, Jesus also said: "Thy sins be forgiven thee". In other words, there were spiritual factors contributing to that illness. He needed the ministry of forgiveness with all its healing power too.

As those who study illness today can confirm, emotional and spiritual dis-ease may well express themselves in physical ill- health. It was of the essence of the attitude of Jesus to people and their needs to want not only to make them physically well, but also to mend their broken hearts. Jesus, in his compassion for people, sought to make them *whole*. That was love in action.

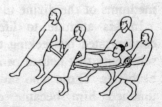

* The healing ministry is further discussed in Numbers 98, 99 and 100

A Positive Faith

"The strength of gentleness" is, Paul tells the Galatians, "one of the fruits of the Spirit". Other evidences of that same "harvest of the Spirit" (as William Barclay translates the phrase) are love, joy, peace, patience, goodness and faith.* These are creative qualities. They declare that real, vibrant Christianity is always expressed in *positive* ways.

We need positive forces in a world dominated by negative, degrading and destructive attitudes. Relationships — be they individual, national, cultural, international and sometimes even ecclesiastical — are damaged by greed, violence, racial prejudice, the violation of creation and other modern obscenities. Starvation on the current vast scale is, in part, the product of wars, ruthlessness, selfishness and corruption. When so much that is negative is infecting the atmosphere, the churches dare not, by what they do or fail to do, add to the negative tone of our times. They must, on the contrary, enable people to find life in its fullness and wholeness.

Jesus underlines the positive nature of the divine intention in his own glorious statement in John's Gospel: "God sent not His Son into the world to condemn the world; but that the world through Him might be saved". God's concern is not with judgmentalism and condemnation, but with salvation. Everything God does is intended to create, re-create, redeem and renew. How then can Christians be negative, arrogant, dogmatic or exclusive — yet still claim to be the mediums of the divine message to the world?

In his attitude to life and to people, Jesus always concentrated on seeking to make them whole. It was his sensitivity that helped people not only to feel better, but to be better. Those who saw him, met him, heard him and touched him became different people. All this he accomplished by his attitude to them. He not only listened to them but also heard them. He not only looked at them but also took notice of them. He not only recognised their pain but also ministered to them.

Christianity is positive or it is nothing. "Negative Christianity" is a self-contradictory phrase. If the church is to reflect the attitude to life and people which Jesus had, it must make known and available the divine grace which "makes all things new". Those who "have been with Jesus" will therefore radiate goodness and gentleness, understanding and encouragement, hope and love, to all. Such positive qualities are, indeed, "the harvest of the Spirit".

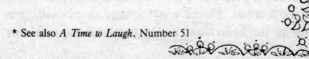

* See also *A Time to Laugh*, Number 51

Go Forward!

Dr Winifred Rushforth was a remarkably gifted doctor and psychotherapist. When I last saw her in her Edinburgh home, she was 93, full of life and working hard. Still seeing her clients regularly, she was also interested in group work. Indeed, as I recall, she was in her seventies when she became involved in encounter groups and went on to lead them with skill and sensitivity. Dr Rushforth told me that she was also working on her next book but was finding progress difficult. "There is so much to do," she said, and then added, to my astonishment and delight, "and I have only ten working years left."

If life begins at 40, it is inspiring indeed to know it can still be productive at 90. What a thrilling experience it was to find such a wonderful commitment to life. Her *joie de vivre* is an encouragement to all of us.

Within the theological verities which constitute our "deep roots and firm foundations", there is much sense of encouragement. "Speak unto the children of Israel, that they go forward" was the divine exhortation to a downcast people. "Launch out into the deep" was Jesus's directive to very sceptical disciples. In the great Johannine statement on the meaning of the Incarnation, the divine purpose is shown to be not discouraging but encouraging: "God sent not his Son into the world to condemn the world". He came that it "might be saved". When the disciples trembled about the future without the Lord, they were encouraged by a promise: "You shall receive power". The Holy Spirit, which would be given to them, would in fact be "another Comforter" not only soothing their pain but bringing them fortitude, strength and encouragement. There was a time when, as recorded in the first book of Samuel, David was "greatly distressed", his womenfolk having been taken as captives by the Amalekites but, we are told, "David encouraged himself in the Lord his God". Within that sentence there lies the ministry of encouragement.

Encouragement should be the hallmark of the caring community. Every member has the right to expect, in their times of wretchedness and dereliction, support and encouragement. Strangely, the church often fails in this ministry, perhaps because it finds it difficult to acknowledge weakness. Church members often find encountering human weakness a problem (as they do accepting the possibility of human weakness in their priest, pastor or minister) but how can caring begin if sharing is not allowed?

There is, secondly, a need to encourage ourselves. It is right to expect care from others but that does not take away the obligation on us to get up from our depths, go on and fight again. Too often we seek refuge in self-pity, defeatism and resentment when we are facing the darkness. While we cannot (as too many wrongly suggest) *will* ourselves out of our depression, we can consciously seek the strength to cope with it. Such self-encouragement is a necessary ministry to ourselves.

Third, David found strength in the resources of his faith. God, as his experience told him, would not let him down. We too have the tools of encouragement in the spiritual resources that are founded on the great sequence of the saving acts of God in Jesus, the crucifixion, the descent into the dark places, the resurrection, the ascension and the sending of the Comforter Spirit. It is a tale of triumph and of victory, a story of profound hope. Surely therein lies "encouragement in the Lord".

Ministry in Print

I was 10 years old when my first journalistic effort appeared in *The Children's Newspaper*. The postal order for 2s 6d that came as a reward, while exciting, was less important than the encouragement I received to undertake a lifelong journey in "the ministry of print". The ministry of Word and Sacrament, expressed through preaching and teaching, has been and remains of prime importance; but the printed word, too, is an essential element in the communication of the Gospel today.

"Letters mingle souls," wrote John Donne. Paul, from the beginning, used the "epistle" to proclaim the message, present his theology, proffer pastoral counsel to the young churches, offer a Christian apologetic. His letter to the Romans remains a formidable theological document. All kinds of pastoral concerns were dealt with in his epistles — sexual immorality in Corinth, confusion in Thessalonica over the second coming of Jesus, the meaning of humility in his epistle to the Philippians.

"The great art o' letter-writin'," (as Sam Weller described it) must not be sacrificed to the technological age, for it can be a medium of comfort and consolation to many. It also allows, to those who find face-to-face exchanges difficult, a way of expressing deep feelings. So important is the place of a letter that the instinctive urge to send one should rarely be resisted. How often we regret that, when we were moved to compassion and "meant to write", we failed to do so. We missed the opportunity to convey a blessing. That opportunity rarely returns.

It is the calling of evangelists to change people, but there are times when the best possible ministry is to recommend a book. How often there is a particular one that has the capacity to minister to the soul, stimulate the intellect, touch the emotions. Sad it is, therefore, that the current economic climate is restricting the availability of books. John Ruskin, in another age, wrote: "What do we, as a nation, care about books? How much do you think we spend altogether on our libraries, public or private, compared with what we spend on our horses?" Change "horses" to "cars" and the question remains.

The need to feed minds, meet emotional needs and nourish souls is a primary concern of communication. The ministry of print, the writing of a letter, the publishing of a book, composing a poem — all these indeed can be tools of evangelism today, essential elements in communication.

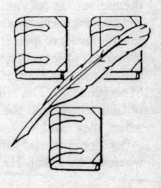

Divine Empathy

The capacity of Jesus to empathise with people in need was remarkable. It did not matter who they were or from what background they came. The common people heard him gladly, but so did an educated intellectual like Nicodemus. A blind beggar could cry from the roadside and be heard. The Syro-Phoenician woman, symbolically scrambling for the crumbs falling from the table of the privileged, could compel his interest and earn his commendation. He was equally at ease with a loathed tax-gatherer like Zacchaeus and an unknown woman of Samaria. His was indeed the divine empathy that characterised the attitude to life and people which Jesus had.

There was similarly the woman who, suffering from a long-standing haemorrhage, sought to "touch the hem of his garment", knowing that even that limited contact would heal her. It did, but not before Jesus had made sure he knew who had touched him. Healing is not magic. It takes place within a relationship. Jesus had to know her in order to heal her. In doing so, he did a significantly important thing. He showed she mattered. She had value.

The ability of Jesus to make people feel important was one of his outstanding contributions to caring ministry. So often then, and even more so now, too many people regard themselves as of no value, despising, rejecting and condemning themselves. The only way to a breakthrough with them is an act of love. It was, even more than his words, the loving *acts* of Jesus that showed his empathy. He understood and shared pain as he does the individual and corporate hells of people today. For, after all, he suffered the inner torment of Gethsemane and the physical agony of Calvary. He "sat where they sat."

God does not send suffering. He sits with us whenever and wherever we suffer. He is the God who shares our pain —

be it physical pain, the emotional pain of rejection, the spiritual pain of persistent failure, the hurt of redundancy and employment. God is not present in pious platitudes about "growing through suffering" (though people do). He is simply there, offering the divine empathy with human agony, individual or on the massive scale of modern times. This caring, loving concern is the attitude to life and people that Jesus had. Must not the disciple be as his or her Master?

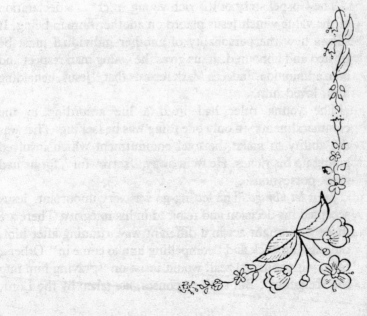

Due Respect

We live at a time when, sadly, respect is a universal casualty. Respect for property and others' possessions diminishes as vandalism increases. Respect for old age is seriously lacking. Areas of life which are properly private and intensely intimate are subjects for public entertainment. Intrusion into private grief is all too common. The amount of violence and death on our television screens speaks of the contemporary lack of respect for human life. God is presented as a figure of fun in a society which is no longer in awe of the divine. Inevitably, respect for people is a casualty too in a world which is often ruthless and very de-humanising.

One of the attitudes to life and people which Jesus had was shown by the respect he had for people, irrespective of their social background or country of origin. It is an attitude much needed in our world today.

The Gospel story of the rich young ruler* is a declaration of the value which Jesus placed on another human being. It shows how the personality of another individual must be treated and honoured. Jesus gives the young man respect and even admiration. Indeed, Mark records that "Jesus, beholding him, loved him".

The young ruler had lived a life according to the commandments. In only one thing was he lacking. That was the ability to make the total commitment which involved giving up his riches. He went away, "sorrowful", for he had great possessions.

Jesus let him go. The letting-go was very important. Jesus accepted his decision and rejoiced in his integrity. There are those who might act in a different way, running after him, pulling him back and "compelling him to come in". Others, filled with spiritual zeal, would insist on "praying him into the Kingdom". But such responses, *not* taken by the Lord, deny the respect which is due to those with whom we might disagree, but who have complete integrity. Jesus, by letting the young man go, was offering us all a lesson in how we are to treat each other. For though we may each travel our own way, we are all made in the image of God, and must respect each other.

If people really matter, our attitude to them must be of the kind which Jesus had. A world based on that kind of due and loving respect would be a less intolerant place.

* I have mentioned the rich young ruler several times in these Meditations. It is a story that says a great deal

Acts of Love

The recorded words of Jesus include the most comforting invitation ever given: "Come unto me, all ye that labour and are heavy-laden, and I will give you rest". He was, however, confronting too, as those who experienced his anger learned when, by their dubious commercialism, they turned "a house of prayer" into "a den of thieves".

These two examples illustrate the attitude to life and people that Jesus had. His was the gentlest of ministries when he was face to face with human suffering. When however he encountered spiritual arrogance, religious intolerance, blatant self-righteousness or, as in the Temple incident mentioned above, the prostitution of holy things, he was ready to confront whoever demonstrated wrong attitudes.

Even his disciples could not escape his anger when, by their spiritual blindness, they obstructed his mission. It was to Peter, conceivably his closest colleague, that he had to administer severe criticism: "Get thee behind me, Satan; for thou savourest not the things that be of God, but those that be of men".

Speaking the truth in love is, according to the New Testament, an obligation on Christians. Jesus did just that to (as we have seen) the rich young ruler, but he loved him in doing it. Confrontation as well as comfort is an act of love.

There are therefore times when it is one of the obligations of love to confront people ... perhaps within the family, where wrong policies are damaging the community, over cruelty to human beings and animals or in face of commercial ruthlessness. If people really matter, those who harm and hurt them must be confronted.

Luke's Gospel contains a story to which I have referred in an earlier Meditation.* It illustrates dramatically that there is a time to comfort and a time to confront. It is in Luke, chapter

7, and it contains a glorious "divine surprise". It is the officially righteous Simon, the Pharisee, whom Jesus confronts with the damning words: "Simon, thou gavest me no water for my feet, but this woman hath washed my feet with her tears, and wiped them with her hair". The comfort and the commendation go to the "woman of bad reputation" whose love will be spoken of for all time for "she loved much".

If people are truly important, we shall comfort them in their need and confront them, with humility, when they are wrong. Either way, if we are to reflect the attitude to life that Jesus had, we must act in love.

* See also *Acceptance*, Number 40

Divine Surprises

The Gospels contain many tales of the unexpected. Jesus constantly produced "divine surprises" for both his enemies and friends by his answers, actions and reactions. Incidents on which we have reflected in this series of Meditations on "the attitude to life and people that Jesus had" illustrate that surprise element. The stories of "the woman taken in adultery", "a woman of bad reputation" who washed Jesus's feet with her tears in what he himself described as a never-to-be- forgotten gesture, Simon, the Pharisee, whose meal she invaded to express her devotion to Jesus, the woman of Samaria — all these situations included elements of the unorthodox. It was the surprise factor in them that pointed up an aspect of the truth.

The ninth chapter of Mark's Gospel provides another example of the unexpected. Again it was the disciples who were taken by surprise. They had encountered a man who was "casting out devils" in the name of Jesus and had no doubt as to how they should deal with him. "We forbade him," John reports, "because he followeth not us." There was, however, no approving nod from Jesus for their action. "Forbid him not," he said, adding that anyone doing miracles in his name was unlikely to "speak evil" of him. "He that is not against us is on our part," he added.

The disciples' reactions and those of Jesus highlight the basic difference in their attitudes. His was one of inclusiveness, but theirs was one of exclusiveness. That flexibility "round the edges" of Jesus's stance is crucially important in determining the kind of attitude Christians should have to others.

There is a New Testament passage in which Peter declares that "there is none other name under heaven ... whereby we must be saved". This leads Christians to have a "Christ-centred" stance, but there is nothing in holding that conviction which needs to be translated into dogmatism, intolerance or exclusiveness. Since Paul reminds us that we "only see through a glass darkly", it is unwise to be inflexibly dogmatic about the truth.

Jesus's attitudes reflect the mind and heart of a God of love. The words to which we have been drawn in the way Jesus dealt with people are sensitivity, understanding, empathy, inclusiveness and, of course, love itself. They sum up the attitudes to which disciples, now as then, are committed in everything they do and are.

The Gift of Wholeness

"Do you really want to be well?" This penetrating question was asked by Jesus of a man who had been ill for 38 years. In the *Authorised Version* of the Bible it reads: "Wilt thou be made whole?" (John, chapter 5, verse 6), but the form of the question from a modern version increases its relevance. It is a question to be taken seriously by all who have to deal with personal and pastoral problems. Do those who seek help really *want* to be made well, or do they — for whatever reason, conscious or unconscious — need to hold on to their illnesses?

The question seems, at first sight, to be a rhetorical one. "Who wants to be ill?" most people would ask. The truth is, however, different. Illness can be a weapon in unhappy lives. It is used in some situations for manipulative purposes. It may also become a desperate method for attracting "tender, loving care" by those who, overwhelmed by lifelong loneliness, never manage to attract love from anybody. Illness can be a crutch which we dare not let go. Both carers and the cared-for need to be aware of the subtleties of this question put to the "impotent" (that is, the powerless or paralysed) man who was never able to get into the healing pool at Bethesda.

Jesus's attitude to life and people in relation to their "health" meant that he did not only heal bodies; he mended broken hearts. He offered people peace of mind. He went even further and gave them forgiveness where it was needed. In other words, he sought to make people *whole*. It is in the offered gift of wholeness that we sense the profundity of his loving attitude to people and their needs. He offered them life with all its creative potential.

The church's pastoral ministry must be based on the attitudes of its Lord. Caring, loving concern, expressed in a longing to bring wholeness to all people, needs to be at the heart of contemporary ministry. This is the Word *in action*.

If we take seriously the attitude to life and people which Jesus had, we will make proclamation and pastoral care central to evangelism today. He not only preached the Gospel with boldness, but made it real and relevant in his loving compassion for a suffering world. His disciples must "go and do likewise".

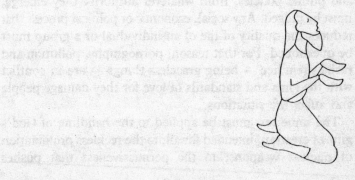

Graceless Things

The word "grace", in its everyday sense, suggests charm and elegance. In its New Testament sense it relates to the goodwill, favour and undeserved blessings that come from a loving God. It therefore points to that which uplifts, transforms and renews people. Grace revitalises, invigorates and regenerates the inner life and is "good". That which diminishes, degrades, defiles, distorts and thereby damages our spiritual welfare must be classified as "evil".

William Barclay, in his translation of the New Testament, provides a remarkable version of Paul's Hymn of Love in I Corinthians, chapter 13. I have always admired his rendering of verse 5: "Love doth not behave itself unseemly". He offers a moving, dramatic version: "Love never does the graceless thing".

Gracelessness characterises all that degrades rather than enhances; that demotes rather than lifts up; that leads to spiritual deterioration rather than growth. Love cannot therefore be associated with "graceless things". Whatever inhibits spiritual progress; whatever has a deleterious effect on behaviour and personality has no part in love's programme. Love cannot countenance the things that destroy the soul.

Here then is a principle by which both personal behaviour and public policies, from whatever authority they emerge, must be judged. Any social, economic or political process that reduces the quality of life of an individual or a group must be questioned. For that reason, pornography, pollution and racial prejudice — being graceless things — are in conflict with the aims and standards of love for they damage people and affect life situations.

The same test must be applied to the handling of God's gifts of creation, intended for all; to the reckless proliferation of nuclear weapons; to the permissiveness that pushes standards beyond the limits in the name of forward thinking; to deficiencies in industrial relationships; to the problems of medical ethics.

If whatever is presented as a policy does not contribute to the good which God wills for all his children; if it affects negatively the physical, mental, emotional or spiritual health of people, it is in conflict with the greatest principle of all, the principle of love. Those whose lives are shaped by a religious faith have a responsibility to contribute to the welfare of humanity through the positive, creative gifts of grace. Those whose primary concern is to bring some measure of "life abundant" into the world want no association with graceless things.

Be Encouraged!

Nehemiah was a cup-bearer in the palace of King Artaxerxes when God "put it into his heart" to do something for Jerusalem, the city of his forefathers and his spiritual home. He had heard, in exile, that it was broken down and desolate. With the king's permission, he set off for the holy city, obedient to the divine prompting that he must rebuild the walls of Jerusalem.

When Nehemiah reached the city, he found chaos. The walls were broken down and "the gates consumed with fire". He went out by night to survey the destruction and found he could not even find places for his ass to walk. The task was far greater than he had ever contemplated, but he refused to be discouraged by its magnitude. "The God of heaven, he will prosper us," he told his companions with conviction, "and we his servants will arise and build."

It is part of the ministry of encouragement, laid on us all, to help people to accept whatever situation they face as Nehemiah did, and to ensure that they understand the realities of it. Whether we are dealing with our personal inner problems, contemplating the difficulties faced by the churches in engaging in evangelism in an excessively materialistic world or simply seeking to be (in Paul's words) "obedient to the heavenly vision", acceptance of the facts, positively not reluctantly, is the only valid launch-pad for "new creation".

I noticed that the piano tuner had only two stumps on his right hand. Six days before the end of his military service, an accident when working on a tank removed two fingers completely and half of each of the other two. The young professional pianist's playing days seemed to be over. He applied for a job as a piano tuner and was accepted, but he was not satisfied. Refusing to pity himself, he took stock of the realities of his predicament, then determined to be a pianist again. He succeeded. Using the two stumps on his right hand skilfully and over-working his left, he learnt to play *his* way. The classics were out of the question, but pop music was not. He was a professional pianist once more, and has been ever since.

The pianist, like Nehemiah, accepted the things which could not be changed but did wonders with what could! Be encouraged by their example to "go and do likewise"!

A Giant of Faith

Nehemiah, as we have seen, was a man of faith, courage, penetrating insight and profound spirituality. Called by God to rebuild the walls of Jerusalem, he carried out his task on principles and policies which, translated into the needs of contemporary mission, have much to say to today.

Nehemiah's prime purpose was to carry out the work through the people who were there. "The God of heaven, he will prosper *us*," he declared, "therefore *we* his servants will arise and build." It was "the locals" who must rebuild the walls. It is, similarly, Christ's people on the spot who are the agents of mission today. If the local church is not positively proclaiming the Gospel, demonstrating the meaning of loving fellowship and offering compassion and care to the community in which it is set, it is effectively "null and void".

The second aim was to use everyone's diverse abilities in the operation and so some built, some fetched and carried, some acted as guards. What was important was that everyone should pool their gifts for the common cause. So must it be today. Some must preach, some teach, some sing, some administer. But there are also less public gifts which are important too — the capacity for friendship and healing relationship, a sense of humour, the ability to cater, for did not somebody lay the table for the Last Supper and so contribute mightily to Jesus's mission?

Nehemiah reminded them too of the danger of separation. "The work is great and large," he pointed out, "and we are separated upon the wall, one far from another." It is the same in evangelism. Mission and unity go together, for unnecessary disunity is damaging to the cause.

Above all, the task was encompassed in prayer. "I prayed to the God of heaven," says Nehemiah, and in doing so emphasises the truth which needs to be remembered today.

"Except the Lord build the house, they labour in vain that build it." God is the source, we are but channels.

Infinite Love

Wilt thou forgive that sin, where I begun
Which is my sin, though it were done before?
Wilt thou forgive those sins through which I run
And do them still, though still I do deplore?
When thou hast done, thou hast not done —
For I have more

The pain of confession and the plea for forgiveness in John Donne's *Hymne to God the Father* will find a response in those who similarly suffer an over-whelming sense of guilt and cry out for re-assurance. Others might feel that the presentation of the Gospel by some preachers and evangelists puts too much emphasis on the creation of guilt feelings in leading people to "decision" and "surrender".

Confession, in that it is "good for the soul" is healthy, but concentration on guilt (for it is often complicated by "unconscious" factors) can create such a sense of personal unworthiness that anxiety, fear, "nervous breakdown", inability to cope and even suicidal feelings can result.

"The eternal verities" include, as I have said earlier, the doctrine of forgiveness. It is in the Apostles' creed because it is of the essence of the faith. Practised as well as proclaimed by Jesus, it is the heart of the Gospel, as both "the woman taken in adultery" and the one of "bad reputation" who washed his feet with her tears, discovered. From ecclesiastical representatives, they had received only hostility and condemnation; from Jesus they experienced acceptance and love. They left comforted.

Paul, in his dramatic confession of inner failure ("the good that I would, I do not and the evil which I would not, that I do") certainly reflected the feelings of John Donne. His answer to his spiritual dilemma was a triumphant cry: "Who shall deliver me from this body of death? I thank God through Jesus Christ our Lord". It is the reality of forgiveness, as part of God's infinite love, that makes people feel better and be better.

Guilt is a valid and necessary feeling. When we hurt someone by word or action, we ought to feel guilty and seek forgiveness. We are bound to share in corporate guilt over our part in the failures that produce war, racism, pollution and starvation. So long as guilt is "appropriate", it is proper and right. There is however "inappropriate guilt" which is a "neurotic sense of guilt over those experiences of feeling guilty which are not explicable in terms of the patient's conscious values" (Charles Rycroft).

It is simplistic to assume that declarations of forgiveness can dispose of complicated psychological problems. Nevertheless, the transforming power of grace and love can reach the inner hidden depths in ways difficult to define. It is, therefore, always relevant to bring the forgiving love of God into situations wracked by guilt.

To those who say with John Donne "But I have more", the New Testament responds "*My grace is sufficient for you*".

Many Ways to Faith

It is part of the wonder of religious faith that God reveals Himself in many-splendoured ways. Variety, rather than uniformity, characterises the Divine activity. In speaking of the gifts of the Spirit, Paul confirms this: "There are different kinds of gifts, but the same Spirit gives them all". What is important is that the mark of the Spirit is not sameness, but difference.

Because of this, it is arrogant for anyone to claim that what they assert or do is alone "the will of God". A true spirituality never claims that (adapting some words from Isaiah) "my ways must be God's ways and my thoughts God's thoughts". The Holy Spirit, Jesus tells us, like the wind, "blows wherever it wishes". The Spirit cannot and must not be imprisoned within human concepts. Faith is therefore more expressed in freedom than in limitation, in inclusiveness rather than exclusiveness. This does not mean that inclusiveness has no boundaries, that it is open to anything and everything. To be "conformed to this world" would end up as licence rather than responsible liberty in Christ.

While Christians must be united on the great foundational verities of the faith, there should be ample opportunity for varying expression of it. In worship, for example, it is a privilege to share varieties of religious experience — emphasis on preaching as in my own Church of Scotland tradition, the glorious programmes of music related to worship in Anglican cathedrals, the singing of the Methodists, the silence of the Quakers, the "enthusiasm" of a congregation charismatically renewed, whether Roman Catholic or Protestant, the elaborate liturgy of the Eastern Orthodox churches, the evangelical simplicity of some small independent group. The variety and diversity characteristic of the Spirit's activity, provide what human beings need, the opportunity for different kinds of people to share worship, liturgy and fellowship appropriate to their temperaments.

Communication is too often aimed at the intellect and forgets the imagination. Music, art, poetry and indeed the whole range of the creative arts offer profound ways of reaching the needs of the soul and spirit. Meditation, contemplation and (to those so gifted) mysticism are means through which, as the Psalmist says, "deep speaks to deep".

So many-splendoured are love, worship, the gifts of the Spirit and even God that there must be an infinite variety of ways in which we communicate the faith to the changing world of today.

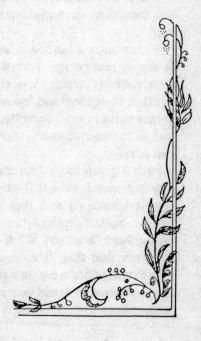

Committed to Care

There are times when communication is not a matter of "talking at" or "doing to". It is a matter of "being with". The doctrine of the Incarnation is a theological statement about "being with". Jesus would be called Emmanuel because, says Matthew, it means "God with us". Throughout his mission, Jesus was indeed God present with people, however awful their situation. That presence was a healing presence.

Jesus's ministry to Zacchaeus is a model for pastoral caring. It represents a "moving towards" in compassion ("Today, Zacchaeus, I am coming to your house") and then a "being with" in a sharing of his misery. The result was Zacchaeus's public statement of regret and commitment to restitution.

This is an example of redeeming relationship in action, a true communication of the grace of God to someone in deep need.

Within such a healing relationship there is a *commitment* to *sharing* and *caring*, three words which aptly describe the life of the early church (Acts, chapter 4, verses 31-37). Meeting together in worship and fellowship, the church showed itself to be a community committed to sharing and caring ("they had all things common ... and parted them all, as everyone had need").

Such a group had a dramatic effect on the world to which they witnessed for 3,000 were converted in one day. The apostles' teaching and preaching had contributed to this success, but the depth of their fellowship and the level of their caring was a factor too. What they *did* was wonderful. What they *were* said that "they had been with Jesus".

St Francis once went on a preaching mission, taking with him a novice who would benefit by the experience. The latter, on his return to the monastery, was bemused. "I thought we

were going on a preaching mission," he said. "We did,"
replied Francis. "But you never preached to the people at
all. All you did was minister to people with help and comfort."
"Exactly," said St Francis. "We preached in the comfort we
offered and in the love we showed. *We preached as we went.*
It was thus we preached."

So do we all. The healing presence of another, whether
spoken words are used or not, is in its commitment to caring
and sharing, a prime means of communication.

Spread the Word!

Broken relationships, at international or national levels, usually begin with a loss of communication. Equally, in personal relationships, it is a sure sign of potential marital breakdown when people can no longer talk to each other about elements that threaten their marriages. Such a loss of verbal communication is, moreover, symptomatic of a loss of contact at deeper levels. Words alone, however, cannot heal such broken relationships.

"Come, let us reason together," God says to His people about their relationship with Him, damaged by their sin. "Let us argue it out," as the *New English Bible* translates that sentence in Isaiah. The restoration of relationships is, however, much more than a matter of reasoning and discussion. For people or groups who have lost touch with one another (a significant phrase), verbal communication is just not enough.

How do we communicate the unchanging Word to a rapidly changing world? It is Paul who asks the relevant question: "How shall they hear without a preacher?".

Ordination is to the ministry of Word and Sacrament. The primacy of preaching is symbolically represented in some traditions by the centrality of the pulpit in churches. But for those traditions which make central the altar or communion table, there remains for all who are ordained a firm commitment to preaching and proclamation.

Many today feel that preaching, as it is traditionally understood, is out-of-date and irrelevant; that "dialogue" is more important than "monologue"; that an experiential approach to communication is the only relevant way. But other forms of communication, however valuable in themselves, cannot be substitutes for that which Jesus specifically exhorted his disciples to do, that is to "go into all the world and preach the Gospel to every creature".

The formation of the Christian community from the beginning was based on the command of Jesus to his followers to preach and heal. The disciples' response, as the book of Acts records, was to "speak the word of God with boldness". Down through the ages, the practice of preaching has been consistently maintained. Whatever additional forms of communication are needed to convey the wonder of the Word to a constantly changing world, evangelism will lose an essential tool if the proclamation of the Word ceases to be a priority today.

The Ministry of Touch

For wonderful language and dignity of expression, nothing surpasses *The Authorised Version* of the Bible. Other translations are, however, valuable as aids to understanding the Word.

Occasionally, one of the more recent versions touches great heights. In *The New English Bible* I find one such passage — Ephesians, chapter 3, verses 14-19. It offers a gloriously moving translation:

> *I kneel in prayer to the Father, from whom every family in heaven and on earth takes its name, that out of the treasures of His glory He may grant you strength and power through His Spirit in your inner being, that through faith Christ may dwell in your hearts in love. With deep roots and firm foundations, may you be strong to grasp, with all God's people, what is the breadth and length and height and depth of the love of Christ, and to know it, though it is beyond knowledge. So may you attain to fullness of being, the fullness of God Himself.*

Reflect quietly on these words and phrases: "deep roots and firm foundations"; "to know" that which is "beyond knowledge"; "strength and power through His Spirit in your inner being"; "the treasures of His glory". Language like this takes us into that realm in which it is the church's function to lead us ... the spiritual dimension. It is "communication" that reaches the deepest levels of the inner self. It touches a spiritual nerve and, when that happens, people are changed, converted, transformed, renewed.

In our reflections on the responsibility we have for helping the unchanging Word to reach, touch and affect this changing world, we have pondered on the priority of preaching and the ministry of print in enlightening the mind, "being with" rather than "talking to" as ministry through healing relationship, music, poetry, art and other creative ways of stimulating the imagination. There must, however, also be ministry to the physical body. That involves the ministry of touch. It was something Jesus used frequently and effectively. It remains an essential element in communication today.

The ministry of healing unites all four elements. In the laying on of hands, we have the ministry of touch. The mind is stirred when the Word is proclaimed. Emotional serenity comes when hidden memories are healed. Prayer, which must always encompass healing work, feeds the soul. Healing ministry is then a most important means of communication, for it ministers to the whole person — body, soul, mind and spirit.

161

Back to the Roots

Jesus was a nonconformist (with a small 'n'). He did not speak and act as the kind of Messiah his contemporaries expected. He would not accept as binding legalistic interpretations of ecclesiastical rules and regulations. He was criticised for eating with "publicans and sinners". To engage a female stranger in conversation gave him no difficulty but — especially when the woman was a Samaritan — it puzzled his friends, the disciples. There were many factors involved in the process that led to his crucifixion, but included among them was his unacceptable nonconformity.

The attitude of Jesus to life and people led him into radical action. His radicalism was not however destructive of the law, something of which his detractors constantly accused him. He was in fact "going back to the roots" (which 'radical' means) and interpreting the spirit of the law. The meaning of "sabbath observance" was an example of such an issue between Jesus and his critics. The way in which the scribes and Pharisees expressed the law was not only legalistic and inflexible. It damaged people. Jesus had therefore to go to the "root" understanding of the meaning of the sabbath. "It was made for man's benefit," he told them in effect. "What you are doing is making the needs of man subservient to an institution, the sabbath."

Where institutions, however worthy, however sacred, are made more important than people then religion, like the law, is demeaned rather than honoured.

The attitude and stance which Jesus took on such issues was based on his perception of the divine intention. Precisely because his insights were so clear, because he knew the will of the Father for His people, he never shirked the need to take a stand. His whole life and all his attitudes were determined by his obedience. There was only one thing to which he conformed and that was God's will. That obedience forced him so often to be nonconformist.

The disciple must be as the master who never flinched from the way of the cross, and who refused to conform to human expectations and attitudes in order to escape his inevitable death. It seems, from Acts (chapter four) that the apostles learnt the lesson and made Jesus's attitude their own. Ordered by the magistrates not to speak in the name of Jesus they, too, had to become nonconformists. ''We must obey God rather than men,'' they said. And did.

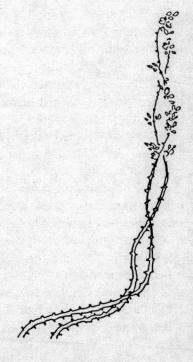

PART IV

TIMES AND SEASONS

A New Beginning

Blessed are those who are given the opportunity of a new beginning! Everyone knows human failure, and the weight of it can be very depressing ... whatever the cause. It may be a broken marriage for which we feel responsible; grief over failures in relationships, personal or professional; the guilt that arises over secret sins and the persistent pressures from within us that tempt us to act out our unacceptable desires. Repeated failure then leads to inappropriate guilt and that can destroy initiative, hope and spiritual enthusiasm, but those with a lively faith should never equate human failure with hopelessness. The doctrine of forgiveness is the very heart of the Gospel. Its product is inner peace.

New life stems (in Emil Brunner's phrase) from "the divine initiative". God is the author of each "new creation". To develop the spiritual life, however, involves an important spiritual law. It is that growth in grace depends on co-operation between God and human beings. The gift is from God but *we* have a crucial part to play.

This law is evidenced in various aspects of the religious life, for example in the practice of intercessory prayer. Our petitions contribute to the possibility of change in people and situations. For that reason, Jesus commands his followers to be "importunate" in prayer. "Pray without ceasing," says Paul similarly to the Thessalonian Christians.

Consider also the sacraments. The efficacy of the sacraments as means of grace depends on various elements — God's repeated promises, the use of the appointed elements and the presence of faith in the recipient. If that last factor is absent, something essential to the sacrament is missing and it cannot fulfil its purpose.

Look too at the ministry of healing. As we contribute to the development of our illnesses, so must we play a part in our healing. God wants us to be whole, but if we are not prepared to change wrong attitudes, habits or lifestyle, our healing cannot be accomplished.

God wills our salvation, our wholeness, but to effect it He needs our obedience, commitment and self-discipline. The opportunity of a new beginning is always on offer and should be gratefully and gracefully grasped. Growing in grace is an exercise carried out in collaboration with God. Out of it, spiritual growth will surely come. When it does, it will be expressed in "the harvest of the Spirit".

Looking Forward

There is a text in the New Testament that comes in Paul's letter to the Philippians and runs: "Forgetting those things which are behind, and reaching forth unto those things which are before, I press toward the mark for the prize of the high calling of God in Christ Jesus". It is a profound statement about the aim, end and purpose of our spiritual journey. It is, in fact, a text for life.

Paul cannot be asking us to forget everything that is in the past. To erase experience, deny tradition, dismiss happy memories or ignore our mistakes would constitute a great loss. What he is seeking to do is to ensure that we get our *perspective on life right*. We cannot change the past, but we can shape the future. It is therefore the part of the journey that is to come that matters most. We must keep looking forward.

In early years and middle age, looking forward is tolerable but for those advanced in years or limited by illness, it can feel very different. It is nevertheless essential that, at whatever stage in life we are, our eyes are facing forward. The encouragement to do this comes from people who, although older, have always looked ahead with enthusiasm. A former Lord Chief Justice of Canada, Sir William Mulock, commented on his 90th birthday: "The best is yet to be, hidden beyond the hills of time". It is life-giving to look forward. Carol Jeffrey, psychotherapist and founder of The Open Way, is looking forward to the publication of her first book — at 93!

Christian hope is not superficial optimism. It is "sure and certain hope", founded on the providence of a God who is active in history and present with us in our suffering. He does make things, especially in answer to prayer, "work together for good". We therefore "press toward the mark", in God's purpose for us, assured that it is not our weak hold on God that is important. It is His "mighty grasp" of us that matters. We are in the hands of a "love that will not let us go". Look forward then ... in confidence and faith.

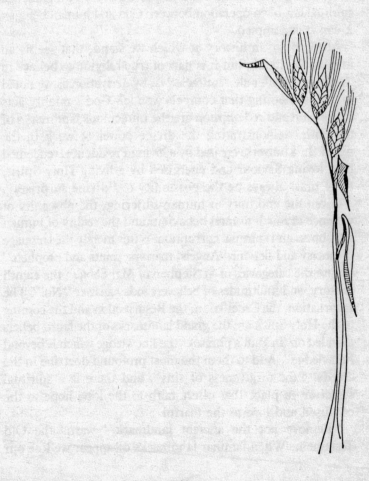

Landmarks of Faith

Many people have told me that they shared the Queen's assessment of her 1992 as their personal *annus horribilis*. The memories of that year will remain, for all experience becomes inextricably woven into the tapestry of our lives. That said, 1992 must now be laid to rest. 1993 must be an *annus mirabilis*, a wonder-full year. With God's help (for there is a fundamental spiritual law of co-operation between God and human beings), it can be attempted.

At the point in history at which we stand, that seems an impossible dream, but it is part of true religion to believe in "miracles". After all, "miracle" is, by derivation as we noted earlier, something that compels wonder. God's mighty acts in creation and redemption are the miraculous landmarks of the faith, demonstrating the divine power at work in the world. In a universe created by a loving Providence, redeemed by a loving Saviour and energised by a living Holy Spirit, there must always be the possibility of "divine surprises".

Given the enormity of human suffering, the obscenity of violence in much human behaviour and the reality of human selfishness and spiritual corruption, is this merely the language of fantasy and fiction? "Angels, martyrs, saints and prophets" (to use the categories of St Stephen of Mar Saba in the eighth century) and multitudes of believers today answer "No!". The Incarnation, the Crucifixion, the Resurrection and the coming of the Holy Spirit are the grand landmarks of the faith, beliefs founded on (in Paul's phrase) "the knowledge which is beyond knowledge". Add to them the most profound doctrine in the creeds, "the forgiveness of sins", and there is a spiritual structure in place that offers faith to the lost, hope to the confused and love to the fearful.

"Remove not the ancient landmark," warns the Old Testament. When familiar landmarks disappear we lose our way. Similarly, when religion loses its markers, spiritual confusion inevitably follows

Sadly, these are the characteristics of our times. In a world that is struggling politically, economically, socially and morally, with consequent disorientation in all these areas, it is the more essential that the Church itself should not — through academic public discussion appropriate in theological circles, but only partly heard, partly understood and possibly misinterpreted — undermine its faith and discourage the faithful. The Church must rather proclaim with "boldness" the "things which it most surely believes".

As the new year unfolds, there is a need to re-establish the landmarks of the faith, for it is in the eternal verities that we can find what the times demand — and I have already mentioned — a sense of direction, a sense of perspective, a sense of adventure and a sense of destiny. With them, and with God's help, we can set out to create an *annus mirabilis*, a year of "wonder, love and praise".

The Divine Humility

It is hard to believe what we read in the twenty-sixth chapter of Matthew's Gospel! He has just described the poignant passover meal of which Jesus partook with his disciples before his approaching suffering. It is a time remembered down the ages in millions of celebrations of the sacrament there instituted when Jesus broke the bread and shared the cup. It was a profoundly moving occasion. But how extraordinary! The incident Matthew next records after the Last Supper is the disciples's discussion about which of them should be the greatest. The response to the divine humility was human arrogance.

Arrogance, whether encountered in politician, preacher or crusading group, is simply unacceptable. If, in an individual, it is unattractive and, indeed offensive, how much more damaging it is when corporately present, for example, in racial or religious prejudice. It reeks of assumed superiority. It is an unpleasant characteristic of people who seek to control, limit or even ban those with whom, or with whose views, they disagree. It is a fundamental aspect of intolerant fundamentalism, of whatever kind. None of these destructive aspects of arrogance should however surprise us, for it is, as the Genesis story makes clear, the primal sin in the Garden of Eden. The tempting serpent appeals directly to human arrogance. "You shall be as gods," he urges. It is that factor that brings about "the fall" and the consequent damage to relationships as it is detailed in Genesis, relationships with God, with others, with the earth, and within ourselves.

"God so loved the world that he gave his only begotten Son" in order to restore a right relationship with Him and consequently with others. The answer to human arrogance is the divine humility, expressed in the wonder of the Incarnation. Jesus (says Paul) "made himself of no reputation and took upon him the form of a servant. (He was) found in fashion as a man. He humbled himself ...". If mere human words can describe divine mystery, this surely proclaims the humility of God.

In washing the disciples' feet, Jesus deliberately demonstrated humility to be the mark of both the individual follower and the church corporate. "The Churches must learn humility as well as teach it," said George Bernard Shaw (in his Preface to *St Joan*). It is a quality that still needs to be proclaimed and practised in high places, ecclesiastical and secular. Certainly there can be no ministry of reconciliation where arrogance is displayed, nor is a ministry of healing possible if those seeking to be channels of God's power lack humility. Those who claim they follow Jesus must, in their self-presentation, relationships and evangelism, be "clothed in the garment of humility".

Lenten reflection will include thanksgiving for him who "really and truly became a servant". How strange it is that those who actually sat with him in that upper room should so soon turn to a selfish and arrogant concern with personal greatness! But, alas, how human!

The Real Lent

Without the falling rain, rivers diminish, mountain streams dry up, reservoirs become empty. Without the gentle breeze or mighty wind, the windmills remain motionless. Without appropriate food and drink, bodily strength falters. Without sleep, energy ebbs away. It is the same in the spiritual life. It can be healthy only if properly nourished. In order to *give out* we must *take in*. Without replenishment in the deep places, our spirituality will be arid and lifeless.

This is a spiritual law which not only prophets and preachers but also every individual will ignore at their peril. If all the emphasis in life is on activity, be it in the personal, corporate or even church spheres, and prayer and stillness are squeezed out, there will be much busy-ness, but little effectiveness. Feverish activity may impress some people, but over-concentration on *doing* seriously damages *being*.

If Jesus himself felt the need for isolation as a preparation for involvement, how much more do ordinary human beings need physical, mental, emotional and spiritual relaxation as a precursor to further endeavour. It is just here that that necessary sanctuary, the "desert place", comes in. The wilderness is the place of preparation, confession and self-awareness of divine grace. Luke therefore records that Jesus returned from the wilderness "in the power of the Spirit".

Lent, says Harry Williams,* "has nothing to do with giving up sugar in your tea or trying to feel it's wicked to be you ... Our Lent is going with Jesus into the wilderness". It is the place of trial and testing but it is also the place of ultimate victory. In that desert place, we encounter ourselves, "warts and all", but in the same moment become aware of the forgiving, renewing, grace-full love of God. It is indeed the place where we *take in*.

Surprisingly, perhaps, it is the Spirit who created Jesus's

wilderness ordeal. Matthew records it thus: "Then was Jesus led up *of the Spirit* into the wilderness". Luke goes further: Jesus was *driven* there by the Spirit. The one who was to give out supremely to the world in words, compassion, love and blood, found in the ordeal of the wilderness, the grace and power he needed to fulfil his mission.

The church exists to forward that mission. It must never then allow itself to be drawn away from its primary task. That responsibility is to offer the bread and water of life to the spiritually hungry and thirsty. If it fails to offer the gifts of grace "in Jesus's name" it will become a sterile, irrelevant and insignificant organisation.

"Accept your wilderness," says Harry Williams. "From the story of the Son of Man, realise what your Lent really means. Then the angels will minister to you as they did to him." Indeed, they will.

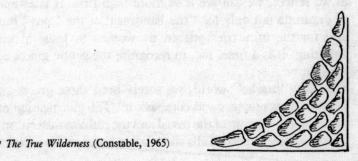

* *The True Wilderness* (Constable, 1965)

The Gentle Graces

It must be a privilege to be called "Mary". To share that name
with the mother of Jesus surely brings the kind of blessing
that comes from contact with real holiness. But there is so
much more to be said. Not only was Mary the most important
person in relation to Jesus's birth but, at his crucifixion (John
tells us) there were *three* Marys (including his mother) present.
Then, when his time for resurrection came, whom did he
encounter in the garden but Mary of Magdala. In other words,
*at each of the great saving acts of redemption for the world, there
was a Mary present. His mother Mary was at the incarnation,
the Marys were at the crucifixion and Mary Magdalene was at
the resurrection.*

Not surprisingly, yet another Mary to whom he was close
(for "Jesus loved Martha and her sister") demonstrated the
spiritual concern that led him to say in commendation: "Mary
has chosen that good part which shall not be taken away from
her".

"You are blessed among women," the angel told the Mary
who was to bear the Son of God. Surely blessed by association
are those who bear the name "Mary" today, for it is a name
that mattered greatly to our Lord.

The fourth Sunday in Lent, Mothering Sunday, is a
thanksgiving for motherhood. And rightly so. But perhaps,
as we reflect, we can see it as more than that. It is a time
of gratitude not only for "the handmaid of the Lord" but
also for the ministries offered by women to Jesus in his
suffering. It is a time, too, to recognise the gentle graces of
femininity.

In this "macho" world, we sorely need these graces ...
sensitivity, gentleness and compassion. The glorification of
violence, the worship of the trivial and the ruthless materialism
that so subtly infects us all, stimulating greed and the desire

for gain, are making our world a darker, more threatening place, a vale not only of tears, but of fears. It is a time to re-establish the strength of gentleness.

The sensitivity and intuitiveness of Mary, the mother of Jesus, the compassion of the Marys who waited by the cross and the tenderness of Mary Magdalene in the Garden of the Resurrection, demonstrate anew the gentle graces of femininity so needed today.

In every human being there are both masculine and feminine components. Although the exact nature of their relationship is unique to each individual soul, there must be a creative balance between them, for it is essential to our wholeness. Let us then be glad that the celebration of motherhood has its place in our real Lent, for it does something to emphasise, to our sad and needy world, the gentle graces of womanhood.

The Will of God

It can be so difficult to discern the will of God. All kinds of pressures, external and internal — self-interest, rationalisation, wishful thinking — impinge on our understanding of God's will and our ability to hold to our conviction. It may, then, be helpful to reflect, in a moment, on an Old Testament cautionary tale.

Mr Bumble clearly did not rate highly the intelligence of an ass! In a withering comment on an expressed legal opinion (in Dickens's *Oliver Twist*), he said (somewhat ungrammatically): "If the law supposes *that*, it is a ass, a idiot". Palm Sunday puts a different value on this (at least in Bible times) invaluable beast. Jesus, consciously and deliberately, chose it to bear him into Jerusalem. The presence of that ass could not fail to make an impact on many, amid the loud hosannas and waving palms. This was exactly what the Old Testament prophet, Zechariah, had foretold: "Behold, thy King cometh unto thee — lowly, and riding upon an ass".

Recall, now, another Old Testament passage, that cautionary tale which brings credit to an ass, this time the one used by Balaam, the prophet. Balak, King of Moab, sent ambassadors to enlist the support of Balaam (*per pro* God) in overcoming his enemy. Balaam, in his second response to the request (we shall return to this) seriously displeased God by his ambivalence over the divine will. He set off with Balak's messengers only to be halted by his beast's refusal to go further. For its assumed stubbornness, it suffered from Balaam's violent temper (his cruel actions suggest an inner turmoil). But what dramatic irony! The prophet of God is blind to "the angel of the Lord" barring his way, while the much-maligned ass is sensitive to and wholly aware of the divine presence!

But back to the story recorded in Numbers, chapter 22.

It focuses on the need accurately to discern God's will and be obedient to it. Balak's representatives had asked Balaam to "curse this people" for "they are too mighty for me". God told Balaam to send them away, saying: "The Lord refuses to give me leave to go with you". In Balak's eyes, however, even a prophet has his price so "more honourable" ambassadors carrying "the rewards of divination" are to be despatched to Balaam. It was no use. "If Balak would give me his house, full of silver and gold, I cannot go beyond the word of the Lord". Well said, indeed! Then comes the fatal *but*. Let me think about it overnight, Balaam says in effect, and I will give you my decision tomorrow. The damage was done. The first judgment had been God's will, the second Balaam's wish. Balaam went with the messengers only to find the angel of the Lord barring his way.

"Jesus set his face to go to Jerusalem." He knew God's will for him. Neither the pain of Gethsemane nor the agony of Calvary would divert him from obedience to his calling. Would that we all had something of that strength when instinctively we know God's will for us.

179

Walking with God

We know little about Enoch, listed in Genesis in "the generations of Adam", but we do know his moving epitaph: "Enoch walked with God".

It was during the Second World War that I had to find an address in an unfamiliar city. Lighting, street-names and careless talk were all forbidden. Directions followed by the inevitable "You can't miss it" failed completely. I could and did. I asked for help a third time and was about to receive yet another set of instructions when the stranger halted: "To be sure you get there safely," he said, "I will go with you".

This story, in itself trivial, is nevertheless a cameo of our spiritual pilgrimage. If, as travellers on life's journey, we feel safe and secure in our destination, it is because (like Enoch) we are "walking with God". The Divine Companion will honour the faith of those who, at his word, "launch out into the deep".

Lent is a time of "commitment to humility and growth in holiness ... an exercise in penitential spiritual renewal", writes David Tripp.* "It is a time of spiritual combat ... characterised by confidence in spiritual victory through grace ... It will be a struggle (but) it represents an opportunity for personal growth". The sense of the presence of God on the stormy journey of life is vital to the development of spiritual maturity.

Growth in holiness involves self-examination, but there is no need for morbid introspection or a surfeit of inappropriate guilt (as distinct from a proper sense of guilt over wrong done). Consciousness of that perhaps over-dramatic phrase (in the letter to the Hebrews) "crucifying the Son of God afresh" may, however, lead to feelings of anxiety over our part, even if it is only by association, in bringing about Jesus's death. What tension there was at the Last Supper when Jesus said to the disciples: "One of you shall betray me"! We are told that "one after another" the disciples mumbled, "Lord, is it I?". Did Peter wonder about his past gaffes and coming denial? Did Thomas sense his inner doubt? And so on, round the table, representing perhaps our own failings and sins.

There is, hidden behind each individual persona (as recent personal tragedies have shown), that side of us which it is hard to acknowledge, our unconscious shadow. Reflection on that part of us is essential and right, even though it may lead us towards despair (as it did Paul). But we need never be overwhelmed. Lent is, as Tripp tells us, "characterised by confidence in spiritual victory through grace".

"O for a closer walk with God", wrote William Cowper. Penitential exercise is a spiritual obligation but it takes place within the assurance of the Gospel promises. Those who walk with God on life's journey are guaranteed forgiveness, renewal and life.

* Taken from 'Lent' in *A Dictionary of Christian Spirituality*, edited by Gordon S Wakefield (SCM Press)

Expectancy

When Jesus was driven by the Spirit into the wilderness immediately after his baptismal experience, he encountered his first spiritual crisis. In Chinese, as I have noted earlier,* the word "crisis" is made up of two ideograms. One means *danger* and the other *opportunity*. The wilderness crisis brought these themes together. There were, Mark reports, the wild beasts, but the ministering angels were there too, present with Christ as he defied the dangers, both physical and spiritual. That he grasped the opportunity to grow in grace through his encounter with temptation is evidenced by his returning into Galilee "in the power of the Spirit". The wilderness was a positive experience through which he clarified the nature of his mission.

If our Lent means going with Jesus into the wilderness, we can expect both testing and triumph. Deep within our inner being, powerful negative pressures, called in religious terms temptations, threaten to break through our defences, seeking to be "acted out" in our behaviour. It is a time of trial and spiritual danger. But because the wilderness is the place where we encounter God and His redeeming love, it is also the place of opportunity. It is in that encounter with ourselves and simultaneously with God that we discover — or rediscover — "life abundant".

Critic and journalist Michael Ignatieff tells us that Winston Churchill called melancholy "black dog" (it is not far from wild beast!). Ignatieff goes on: "These days we all seem to be in black dog's grip. Nations, like individuals, can get it too. The sound I hear around me is a low sigh of despair". Ignatieff is speaking of the prevalent depression that seems presently to be paralysing people and stifling corporate endeavour.

Such depression is very dangerous. It represents a constantly downward spiral. We need, urgently, an upward spiral, and this we will get when we recover that sense of *expectancy* that seems to have so deserted us. Our Lent has within it the opportunity to recover just such expectancy and faith. As Jesus returned "in the power of the Spirit" from the wilderness, so may we through our Lent with him, recover vision and hope.

There is much in the Bible about the spiritual law of expectancy ... in its emphasis on "waiting on God"; in Jesus's instruction to us to ask, seek and knock; in his commendation of the faith of the woman from Canaan who sought her daughter's healing. Jesus created expectancy wherever he went. It is in such situations that miracles happen.

Going with Jesus into the wilderness to share his presence, purpose, power and peace, will lead to our positive return to the world, regenerated, renewed, expectant, grace-full. Lent is not a time for doom and gloom. It is an opportunity to learn — or re-learn — the disciplines of faith and hope.

危机

* See also *Creative Discontent*, Number 21

From Death to Life

The divine humility, so movingly demonstrated when Jesus washed the disciples' feet, is further proclaimed in the event remembered each Palm Sunday, the triumphal entry into Jerusalem. Jesus planned it deliberately to declare publicly his understanding of his Messianic role. Zechariah, the Old Testament prophet, had proclaimed: "Behold, thy King cometh unto thee ... lowly, and riding upon an ass ...". Jesus was entering the city not as a warrior but as a servant.

The spontaneous acclaim given to him by what Matthew called "a very great multitude" simply underlined to the authorities, ecclesiastical and temporal, the threat which Jesus presented, especially if he had the support of "people power". The content of his preaching and the integrity of his practice threatened the spiritual vested interests of the religious leaders. His destruction was essential. As the hosannas of his welcome were replaced by the unfolding events of Holy Week, people power was harnessed to the demand for his death. The shout "Crucify him, crucify him!" rang through the streets.

Jesus, however, had long been aware of the dark face of reality, expressed in conscious hostility to him by his opponents and, more seriously, of the subtle unconscious factors coming from the negative shadow side of his enemies. He accepted the dark face of reality and therefore saw his coming death as within God's will. From the time "he set his face to go to Jerusalem", he knew he must be "obedient unto death".

Each year as we travel through Holy Week, we see anew, with all its frightening intensity, the shadow side of fallen human nature at work. That same negative side of the unconscious — sometimes individual, now collective — has been horrendously demonstrated in events like the bomb in Warrington, despite the severe biblical warning about "offending these little ones". That same shadow is present in power when the people deliberately chose the robber Barabbas and rejected the innocent Jesus.

It is just such an action that sheds light on the sin which is described in the New Testament as "unforgivable". That sin, as the context makes clear, is essentially a state of mind so depraved that it can no longer distinguish between good and evil. The description of Jesus as Beelzebub (a demonic power) is so contrary to the truth that those who made the accusation had reached a condition which is effectively spiritual death. In such a condition repentance is impossible, and without repentance how can there be forgiveness?

The glory of Holy Week is its demonstration of the divine omnipotence. That power is not an ability "to do anything". It is the capacity to take the evil that human beings do and make it praise God. In Holy Week that happens. Out of death comes life. It is there we see the divine humility and the divine omnipotence in concert. Let, then, the people say: "To God by the glory, great things He has done!".

Were you there?

Holy Week begins with joy and ends with victory, but between Jesus's triumphal entry into Jerusalem and the triumph of his resurrection come the sombre events that culminate in his crucifixion. It is not clear that those who welcomed him when he arrived, "lowly and riding upon an ass", knew just why they were cheering. A similar reception, Professor J W Bowman tells us, was given to the pilgrim bands coming from the ends of the earth to worship at the Passover feast. Was it any more than that? Perhaps it does not matter greatly. Jesus knew what he was doing and why. He was presenting an acted parable in terms of Zechariah's prophecy about the humility of the coming King. "Rejoice greatly!" the prophet had said, and so they did with palms and loud hosannas.

Another prophet, Isaiah, in presenting his picture of "the suffering servant", had spoken of him as "despised and rejected of men, a man of sorrows and acquainted with grief". With that image of the Messiah, Jesus identified himself. And so, although "the common people heard him gladly" because "he spoke with authority"; although he had intrigued many with his parables and amazed them with his miracles; although he "went about, doing good", by sharing people's pain and meeting their needs; although he had come, in Ezekiel's lovely words, to "search for the lost, recover the straggler and bandage the hurt", he was dragged before accusers, rejected by the people in favour of the robber Barabbas, made to wear a crown of thorns and compelled to carry his cross to his crucifixion. Why did they do such things to Jesus? What is it in human nature that wants to destroy the good and acclaim the evil? Why do we "crucify the Son of God afresh"? "Were you there when they crucified my Lord?" the old song asks. We were — and, forgive us, we did.

I turn perhaps in an unexpected direction for an insight

into part of the answer. Kenny Everett, usually described as a "wacky" comedian, has — like other homosexual people — suffered abuse and violence because he is "different". A colleague pointed out that others — coloured (as he was), Jewish, the deformed, the ugly — suffer similarly. In a dramatic phrase, Everett commented: "We are receptacles for human hatred". Jesus, "different" because of his holiness and spirituality, was similarly persecuted, vilified, despised and rejected, an innocent receptacle for human hatred, a hatred that is blind, uninformed and wholly unacceptable.

Those who have experienced such abuse may well be comforted by the knowledge that there is a profound divine understanding of what it means and feels like to be acquainted with grief. Can they — and must not we all — be touched by Jesus's attitude to those who planned and executed his crucifixion? "Father, forgive them, for they know not what they do." This surely is the wonder of that love divine, all loves excelling, incarnate in Jesus. Such a capacity to forgive may feel to be far beyond our reach, but it remains the model for us all.

Resurrection Joy

"The Lord is risen, is risen indeed." So the cry of "Alleluia!" rings out in exultation and joy wherever Christians come together on Easter Day. And rightly so. The sad and sombre feelings aroused by the repetition of the journey through Holy Week have given way to a sense of triumph. "Thanks be to God who giveth us the victory through our Lord Jesus Christ!". There may be disagreements among believers on literal aspects of the Resurrection story, but of the reality of his continuing presence as risen Lord, there is no doubt. The Resurrection is a corner-stone of the faith.

Those who today have difficulties in believing that, as The Apostles' and Nicene Creeds assert, "on the third day, he rose again" will feel their doubts were shared even within the circle of the disciples. Perhaps Thomas speaks for many when he records his inability to believe that such an event could happen. I need proof, he cries. And, of course, he is given it. It will not perhaps convince contemporary doubters but it did Thomas. Those who, as Jesus commented, have believed without seeing such proof are blessed, have made an act of faith. That is what believing in the Resurrection is.

Although Jesus had shown himself as risen to various individuals and groups in apostolic circles, there is a sense of uncertainty in the days between Easter and Pentecost. The wrong questions — for example about the restoration of the kingdom to Israel — were still being asked (Acts, chapter 1, verse 6). Nevertheless efforts to stay together and to stabilise the group were made. They maintained their group strength by shared "prayer and supplication". They were "of one accord". "The women, and Mary, the mother of Jesus", were involved in such devotions. The group did necessary practical things like appointing, by lot, a successor to Judas Iscariot in the apostolic band. That mutual support continued until "the day of Pentecost was fully come".

The coming of the Holy Spirit is an event similar in kind to the Resurrection. Belief in that presence is an act of faith. The proof of its reality is the extraordinary effect of the coming of the Spirit on the disciples. A perplexed and puzzled group, holding together — but it feels only just — are transformed into an evangelistic team, ready to take on the world "in Jesus's name". So amazing was the effect that we who claim the name Christians today are such as a direct result of that Pentecost of long ago. To the gathered throng, Peter's proclamation is crystal clear. "God has made that same Jesus, whom you have crucified, both Lord and Christ".

The transformation of the disciples from weak uncertainty to strong conviction and infinite courage is an event that needs an explanation. It cannot lie anywhere other than in the mysterious (in the biblical sense) events of the first Pentecost, the birthday of the church.

It is the Resurrection joy that moves on to the power of Pentecost that is the life-blood of the faith.

The Spirit Comes

I met Canon Andrew Glazewski just once, and that for only one hour, but I recall the occasion with pleasure. He showed me what it means to say: "The Spirit comes!". He died shortly after we met, so I had no opportunity to meet him again. In a snack bar, over a cup of coffee, Glazewski expounded the article in the Church's creed which Pentecost Sunday celebrates: "I believe in the Holy Spirit!".

That doctrine was, for him, rooted in the Old Testament. To show me how, he took a square sheet of paper from his briefcase, folded it corner to corner and then tore it in half, leaving him with two equal triangles. The first he placed, base at the top, pointing downwards; the other he put below it, pointing upwards. The two triangles met at the apexes, looking rather like an angular egg-timer.

Glazewski pointed to the upper, upside-down triangle. That, he said, symbolises the Holy Spirit (it was indeed, "like the form of a dove"). Its ever-widening upward flow suggested the infinity of "grace abounding". The lower triangle, pointing upwards, Glazewski saw as the symbol of human "being". He drew two parallel lines across the triangle, creating three layers. The top area represented the conscious part of personality; the middle layer was that hidden, buried part of us known, in analytical terms, as the (individual) unconscious. (We will come to the third layer in a moment.)

The unconscious (seeking help from a modern analogy) is a recording of all our experiences since birth (and some would also say preceding birth). What is on that tape shapes our adult actions and reactions, determines our feelings and conditions the way we relate to others. Positively, the unconscious is the source of our creativity. Negatively, unhealed hidden feelings exert pressure on us from within and, breaking through, may be "acted out" to our discomfort, unhappiness and even tragedy. Paul knew what this "shadow" side of his nature meant: "The good that I would, I do not; and the evil that I would not, that I do," he confessed.

The third, deepest layer, wider still, is the collective unconscious, that reservoir of corporate conditioning which, for better or worse, contributes to what we are.

"The Spirit comes!" said Glazewski, as he pushed the top triangle slowly downwards to indicate the Spirit's penetration and permeation of our whole being, conscious and unconscious. That transforming, renewing process is salvation at work.

"Look now at the inter-twined triangles," said Glazewski. I did. There was the Star of David!

That is why Jesus came of the Jews, for only the spirituality and depth of their, and his, religion could at that time comprehend what happens when the Spirit comes.

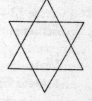

Grateful Remembrance

"Except the Lord build the house, they labour in vain that build it." The words are familiar, but they must not be treated with contempt for they proclaim a profound truth. Those who take no account of the spiritual dimension to life risk failure in all they, as individuals or as citizens, try to do. God must be actively acknowledged in His world.

Our season of Remembrance is a time for gratitude and grief, thanks and tears, but it is, at the same time, an occasion for personal and corporate rededication. There are those who still feel the pain of the First World War, for it cost them the love of their life and therefore the life they would have loved. The Second World War, the Falklands War and the Gulf War inevitably mean for many pride and pain, wounded bodies, damaged minds, longing, loneliness. Grateful remembrance commits us all to the effort to create a fair, just and loving society.

What can happen when God's way is ignored is dramatically illustrated in a short story contained within five verses of Psalm 106, especially when each verse is summed up in a one-word "chapter heading":

Verse 11 — *And the waters covered their enemies; there was not one of them left*. The chapter heading is "Victory".

Verse 12 — *Then believed they his words; they sang his praise*. The chapter heading is "Thanksgiving".

Verse 13 — *They soon forgot his words; they waited not for his counsel*. The chapter heading is "Indifference".

Verse 14 — *but lusted exceedingly in the wilderness, and tempted God in the desert*. The chapter heading is "Sin".

Verse 15 — *And he gave them their request; but sent leanness into their soul.* The chapter heading is "Destruction".

What a storyline! Victory, Thanksgiving, Indifference, Sin, Destruction. What a tragedy! For the story that begins with Victory ends in Destruction.

Why did the story turn towards tragedy? The clue to the answer must lie in the chapter connections. Two are natural enough — Victory to Thanksgiving, Sin to Destruction. One is understandable — Indifference to Sin, for indifference untreated becomes something more negative. The crucial question is: How does Thanksgiving move to Indifference so quickly? But post-war experience twice over confirms how easy it is, in a world dominated by materialism rather than God, to slip from the idealistic visions of victory to individual and corporate indifference.

It is an essential part of grateful remembrance to reassert the primacy of the spiritual dimension to life, that is to ensure that, as our initial text says, God is involved in all our "building", individual, national and international.

The Quiet Mind

Asked to draw or paint a picture of "Peace", the majority of the pupils in a senior class chose to portray landscapes — hills and valleys, meadows and rivers. These are, of course, places of peace. But one girl's picture was different. She painted a city street, crowded with people, jammed with traffic. Above it, on a branch of the tree in the adjacent park, a little bird sang cheerily. It seemed at peace with the world. True peace is of that kind. It is an oasis of calm in a turbulent world.

Such is the quiet mind. It is serenity in the midst of strain.

The importance of the quiet mind was often demonstrated by Jesus. He needed it when he was under pressure from the multitudes seeking his compassion and healing. He showed that attitude when he was facing persecution or under threat of death. Taken before his accusers, he had to face false claims and listen to blasphemies, yet his response was striking. "*Jesus answered them nothing.*" This is the silence of dignity I have mentioned earlier. It is a product of the quiet mind. It is expressed in calmness in the face of trouble, in tranquillity in the face of hostility, and in serenity in the face of tribulation and suffering.

The quiet mind is a gift of grace. We do not ourselves have the resources to create it. It comes as a gift from God. Behind it lies a spiritual perspective, an active sense of the embracing, loving providence of God and a conviction that, as Paul declares: "*Nothing* can separate us" from the Divine Love.

Remembrance Day is the day on which we share two minutes of silence. The noisy, turbulent world pauses to remember with mingled gratitude and sadness, the sacrifices, suffering and pain of two world wars and other conflicts. At the same time, we know that wars and rumours of wars are with us still and, what is worse, in a nuclear age. If we are going to be able to live in and cope with this world of conflict and violence, with the weight of human suffering it contains, we *must* find that inner peace. We must cultivate the quiet mind.

"Wait on the Lord. Be of good courage and He shall strengthen thine heart," the Good Book says. God will do more. If you will receive it, He will give you the quiet mind.

The Healing Light

The Saviour comes! So Advent proclaims that "the people that walked in darkness have seen a great light!". It is the season which announces annually the coming of the Servant-king, in love. He comes to "heal the broken-hearted"; to "preach deliverance to the captives"; to be "God-with-us". The Advent candles symbolise the presence of the light shining in a world of darkness. The Saviour comes to bring (in the words of the title of an Agnes Sanford book) "the healing light".*

The light shines the more brightly because the darkness is so great. In Yugoslavia tanks have trundled along roads trodden by tourists, while the whole land groans under the pain of internecine conflict. In Iraq Kurds huddle fearfully in flimsy tents, desolate and desperate, facing death through hunger and the winter's cold. In Ireland, the passing years bring killing after killing, the searing pain of bereavement numbing those of every faith — and none. The tormented faces and stricken bodies of the starving young and the dying old are there before us on our television screens, victims of hunger, disease, war and inhumanity. How great indeed is the world's darkness!

The psalmist speaks of the darkness "which hideth not from Thee" and claims that "darkness and light are both alike to Thee". God is not only in the light; we encounter Him in the darkness too, he seems to say. But looking at such world situations, dare we talk of meeting God in the darkness?

There is no place in genuine religion for pious platitudes and doctrinaire declarations about growth through suffering, especially if offered by those who suffer little to those who suffer appallingly. Yet somehow Paul can say that "*nothing* can separate us from the love of God revealed in Christ Jesus our Lord".

Paul had a right to speak in these terms. He suffered persecution, peril, imprisonment, beatings, hunger and cold. He knew too the inner darkness which made him cry: "Who shall deliver me from this death?". But it was through his darkness that he learnt the truth about relationship with God. We may lose all sense of God in our darkness, but He never loses touch with us.

> *Let me no more my comfort draw*
> *From my frail hold of Thee;*
> *In this alone rejoice with awe,*
> *Thy mighty grasp of me.***

God is in the light, but in the darkness too. It is there that He offers us "the healing light".

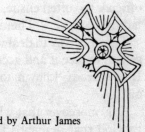

---

* *The Healing Light* by Agnes Sanford published by Arthur James

** An earlier reference to these lines in *The Validity of Prayer*, Number 19

Inner Light

Advent announces the coming of light into our world of darkness. It also brings encouragement to us all as we wrestle with our own darkness. Of our inner conflict, the war between good and evil, we are constantly aware. It is the spiritual dilemma, that battle within which has driven good people into deep depression and some towards "the dark night of the soul". Yet the Gospel truth is that the God whom we encounter in the darkness offers us the gift of inner light.

It needs courage to face the dark, negative side of our being. But the challenge faces everyone for "*all* have sinned and come short of the glory of God". In that we all have a shadow side to our personalities, there is comfort. This spiritual trauma is not unique to us. We are not alone in our darkness.

We need, next, to be aware of the sheer power of that shadow. Whether we speak, as we do in religious language, of "temptation" or, as we do in psychological terminology, of the pressures within us that come from "the unconscious", the experience is the same. The need to "act out" our secret desires can lead us into behaviour unacceptable to church and society. How great then is the condemnation that comes from congregation and community of someone who, with grace and discipline, has "contained" some temptation down the years, but has failed once. Judgment and rejection, personal and official, too often ensue. Yet the only proper response to such failures can be: "There, but for the grace of God, go I".

The only way to deal with that dark side, the unacceptable self, is to face it and accept it, not reluctantly but positively. It is already known to God who accepts us "warts and all".

It is moreover that wholly unconditional acceptance of us by God that demands that we accept others' darkness too. But how can we so love others if we cannot learn to love ourselves? We love our neighbour as we love ourselves.

To acknowledge the reality and depth of our darkness is to open the way to the healing light. The Incarnation is the Good News of the coming of the Light of the World. He comes as love in action to redeem our darkness.

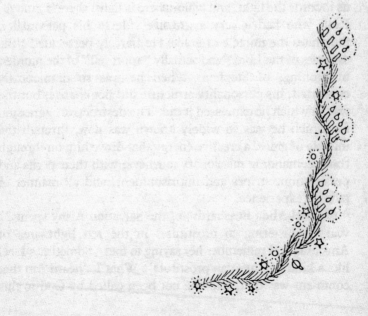

Towards the Light

I remember being taken, when very young, to a cave in the south-west of England. The memory is hazy, but I do recall the bleakness and darkness in the passages leading to the centre of the cavern. Electric light bulbs had recently been inserted into the walls to facilitate safe passage and round each light a hint of green was beginning to appear. I realised then that where there is light and warmth, there is growth.

We meet God in the darkness, communal or personal, for (said the Psalmist) "dark and light are both alike to thee". We have reflected on the need to accept our dark (or shadow) side. Here is further encouragement to do so.

Finding the ability to love our unacceptable self somehow brings the possibility of growth in that area of our being. The "surrender" of our negative side to God creates new possibilities of service. The encounter in the darkness can lead us towards the light; and where there is light, there is growth. Paul, who had a very aggressive side to his personality, illustrates the miracle of grace. He fiercely persecuted "the disciples of the Lord" and actually "approved" of the murder, by stoning, of Stephen. When he was so dramatically converted, his personality structure did not change, but the way in which he expressed it did. The destructive aggression for which he was so widely known was now, through the miracle of grace, a creative energy that drove him on through those demanding missionary journeys, with their perils and persecution, stripes and imprisonment, and all manner of painful experience.

Colonel Alida Bosshardt* of the Salvation Army spent 27 years ministering to prostitutes in the red light area of Amsterdam. I remember her saying to me: "Sometimes I feel like a kind of Christian prostitute". What I "heard" in that comment was that, had she not been called by God to this great ministry, she could easily have become a prostitute herself, because of her need to love and be loved. But then "amazing grace" made her the incarnation of caring love to the hundreds of "red light" girls she knew by name. She gave them love and received back so much from them. The road she took led her to the light; but, unredeemed, she could so easily have gone towards the darkness.

Advent brings the good news of the coming of God incarnate, love in action, leading whoever will towards the light.

* See my reference to Colonel Bosshardt in *The Loving Heart*, Number 31

God with us

Christmas came commercially in October. Christmas comes on to our horizon devotionally this weekend with the celebration of the First Sunday in Advent. We are preparing ourselves for the great event which J B Phillips loved to call "the visit of God". The Incarnation is exactly that for, as John tells us in his Gospel, "The Word was made flesh and dwelt among us". The Good News is enshrined in a name Jesus would be given ... Emmanuel. It means "God with us".

This *is* Good News indeed. It dismisses for ever the picture of God as some distant divine power, dispensing judgment on recalcitrant people. Advent is the announcement of the coming of one who will feel and share all that happens in this "vale of tears". His birth will be lowly, identifying him with the weak and the poor. He will "have no place to lay his head" so the homeless and the refugee will find comfort in that. He will be "despised and rejected of men, a man of sorrows and acquainted with grief" so he can empathise with the isolated, the sad and the bereaved in their pain. He will endure acute suffering of mind, soul and body, so those who are mentally distressed, emotionally wounded or desperately ill will be strengthened by his ability to feel for them. He will meet death when but a young man. The dying, older and younger, will be grateful and glad to know he is "with" them. He is indeed "the man for others", Emmanuel, "God with us".

J B Phillips's faith was founded on the gracious relationship made possible by the "divine initiative," the act of love for which we give thanks in Advent. We love God because "He first loved us" by coming to be "with us" in whatever circumstances we find ourselves, whatever we do. We are in the grasp of a Love that "will not let us go". Phillips wrote: "Christ *is* everything. He is God shown to us in human form. He is God dying a criminal's death to reconcile men and women to himself. He is God triumphing over death. He is God entering human hearts and transforming them from within — a thing unknown in a pagan world either then or now ... God has entered the stream of human history in *person*".*

Advent is for many the promulgation of a great theological doctrine. To others it is a simple (but not simplistic) statement of faith. God is "with us" in loving relationship, to give us the quiet mind, the adventurous spirit, the loving heart. He wills our good. He desires our wholeness. It is Good News indeed.

* From the entry for December 7th in *Through the Year with J B Phillips*, (Arthur James, 1974)

Healing Relationships

It is to a world of broken relationships that Jesus comes with healing power. "God was in Christ, reconciling the world to himself," wrote Paul (to the Corinthians) as he interpreted to them the great saving acts recorded in the Gospels. Christmas is the celebration of and thanksgiving for the Incarnation, the coming of one whose purpose is to heal relationships.

Reconciliation must therefore be the dominant theme in Advent worship, reflection and meditation. The Incarnation is God's reconciling act, an action which commits his servants too to a ministry of reconciliation. God, ourselves and our neighbour are related within a triangle of love, the true "eternal triangle" based (Jesus says) on the greatest commandment of all. Love is at the heart of the Gospel and must therefore be expressed in a commitment to "bind up the broken-hearted", "the bleeding soul to cure"; in other words, to heal relationships.

How timely and relevant is the Advent message! The world hovers on the brink of a horrific war in the Gulf, the result of breakdown in international relationships because of aggression and its consequences. There are wounds to be healed in our national life where prejudice creates inter-group tensions. Negative trends in our society as well as in individuals are the outward expression of the "shadow" within us — materialism, secularism, ruthlessness, selfishness, lust for power, insensitivity. The pollution of the atmosphere and the abuse of creation damage our relationship to the earth. Racial and credal intolerance drives wedges between people and destroys relationships. It is the old, old story encapsulated with dramatic brilliance and to traumatic effect in the Genesis story of the Garden of Eden. There the arrogant disobedience of our representatives, Adam and Eve, distorted their relationship with God and consequently their relationship with each other (mutual blame and resentment), with the earth ("cursed is the ground for thy sake"), and within themselves (guilt).

It is in order to restore a right relationship with God, with ourselves, with the earth and with each other that the child born in Bethlehem became "the man for others" who lived, preached, healed, served, suffered, died and rose again for all humankind.

The Gospel offers reconciliation to a divided world and integration to broken people. It brings Good News for the healing of relationships, through the way of love.

Ecce Virgo
concipiet et
pariet
Filium

The Mystery of Bethlehem

"Let us go even unto Bethlehem and see this thing which is come to pass." The immediate response of the shepherds on hearing the angelic Good News was to hurry to the manger to see the child, born to be "a Saviour, Christ the Lord". Christmas is the season when, in imagination, we are all invited to make that same pilgrimage, there to reflect on "the visit of God", the Incarnation, God-with-us.

The Incarnation is a "mystery", a word which in biblical terms involves two elements, the "secret" plan of God and the medium through whom the secret is revealed. As we encounter this true "mystery", let us reflect on two of the key figures in the story, Mary and Joseph.

Mary — gentle, gracious, intuitive and sensitive — knew that she was part of a mystery. In the Magnificat, her song of praise, she made her statement about obedience and privilege. To Jesus she gave not only a mother's natural gifts. She knew her son was "special" and so whatever he said or did became something over which she would "ponder in her heart". Mary is an inspiration to us all.

Joseph sometimes seems but a background figure, present but unobtrusive. His contribution to the mystery is moving, for his offering was *an attitude of mind*. Reflect on what he was asked to do. The girl he married was already pregnant. That would normally produce anger and rejection in a young husband. The explanation he was given was that his wife was "with child by the Holy Spirit". The only possible response to that would be utter disbelief. Yet Joseph, with extraordinary sensitivity, accepted without question what was happening and sought only to understand his role in what came to be called "the Incarnation". As a result this man of God was full of care for both mother and child, alive to their special needs and acutely perceptive over any threat to the baby Jesus.

Joseph's commitment and faith are a challenge to some attitudes that we may have but need to change.

The mystery of the "divine synchronicity" must move us profoundly for it demonstrates that, "in the fullness of time", Jesus came. Time, geography, the preparation of a people and prophecy combined to make that the moment for "the Word to become flesh". Behind the proper pageantry and celebration of Christmas, there shines out the Good News of the coming of the Saviour in love, his only purpose being the redemption of humankind.

The Choice is Ours

In the divine synchronicity that brought so many factors together so significantly, or as the Bible puts it "in the fullness of the time", Jesus was born in Bethlehem. It had somehow become the place of expectation and seemed to draw so many people, of different kinds, to it.

Mary and Joseph went there for ostensibly practical reasons. "All the world" must be taxed, said a decree of Caesar Augustus and each person had to fulfil the instruction in their own city. At a very late stage in her pregnancy, Mary was taken by Joseph from Nazareth to Bethlehem. But there were deeper reasons. Had not King Herod been told that it had been prophesied that out of Bethlehem would come "a Governor that shall rule my people, Israel"? If the fullness of the time had come, Bethlehem was where Mary and Joseph just had to be.

It was to Jerusalem first and then on to Bethlehem that the so-called "wise men from the East" travelled, having seen the star of "the King of the Jews" appear. Their motivation was clear. They wanted to honour and worship him and they expressed their feelings in the famous and time-honoured gifts of gold, frankincense and myrrh. They were wise indeed. Intuitively they avoided returning to Herod, as he had asked them to do, to protect Jesus, and they journeyed home another way.

Then came the shepherds to Bethlehem "to see this thing which had come to pass". They found themselves in a mystery (in, again, the biblical sense) which they could not comprehend. Carrying out their pastoral responsibilities, they had seen and heard first "the angel of the Lord" and then "a multitude of the heavenly host" announcing the birth of "a Saviour who is Christ the Lord". The days in which they lived and the background from which they came were much more open (in the exact sense) to psychic and spiritual dimensions than our predominantly materialistic atmosphere allows. Aware that something of unusual significance was happening, they immediately left their flocks to go to Bethlehem to see that which "the Lord has made known to us". They moved, we are told, with haste, to find Jesus.

Events in Bethlehem throw into relief two kinds of people, those who have no room for Jesus and those who do. So will it ever be. Discipleship is a free choice. As I have said in another Meditation, God does not bludgeon people into the Kingdom.

The choice then is yours, is ours. Though Jesus seeks people with the cords of love, he is open to rejection still. Those who have no room for him are free to say so — and they will. The fundamental question that is put to each and all is that which was put to Simon Peter so long ago: "Whom do you say that I am?". The response from Peter was: "You are the Christ, the Son of the living God". It was the response only possible by faith. So must that response still be.

Indeed, the choice is ours!

The Energy of Life

"Love," said Robert Browning, "is the energy of life". Henry Drummond, whose spiritual classic *The Greatest Thing in the World* is "an analysis of love," happily made that statement his own. Drummond goes on: "The power to set the world right, to renew the springs of affection, comes from Christ ... The ingredients of love are all in relation to the known today and the near tomorrow, and not to the unknown eternity". The springs of love have their source in the Child of Bethlehem. Jesus was, in a way that only faith can comprehend, "Love incarnate, Love divine".

It was on a garden lawn in Kent that Drummond offered to a gathering of missionaries his spontaneous exposition of Paul's "hymn of love" in I Corinthians, chapter 13. The great evangelist, Moody, was due to speak to the assembled company but confessed to being "tired out with eight months of solid preaching" and introduced instead "a substitute recently returned from Africa, Henry Drummond". Intuitively, the audience realised that it was listening to an historic declaration on the nature of "the spectrum of love" and its ingredients. Later, that address would become a devotional classic as *The Greatest Thing in the World*.

The nine ingredients of love which Drummond presents are one-word summaries of Paul's statements about love. They are patience, kindness, generosity, humility, courtesy, unselfishness, good temper, guilelessness and sincerity. They are to be lived out in the real world on the pattern set by Jesus, Love incarnate.

But the real world we contemplate this Christmas is daunting indeed. Millions starve, Kurds die, Yugoslavia destroys itself, bombs wound and kill, Russians queue for food in freezing cold, cancer claims its huge quota of victims, AIDS' deaths increase, mental illness spreads, children are grievously abused, accident, natural disaster and violence bring bereavement to countless families (including police families). Do words about love have any relevance to all this?

But there is no reason for Christmas without the Child of Bethlehem, the Word become flesh, Love incarnate. His followers have a binding commitment to proclaiming and trying to practise the healing, reconciling, redeeming, renewing power of love. When "Love came down at Christmas," it was in the form of a little child. Three decades or so later, his disciples set out to conquer the world in his name. His followers today have no choice. To proclaim the power of love remains their primary responsibility. The world must learn that love is the energy of life.

Being, not doing

It was late in the afternoon when we motored into Prague. Because of communication failures (this was Czechoslovakia of some years ago), our agent had failed to secure a hotel booking for us. I sought the assistance of the state tourist office, but they were unhelpful and totally indifferent to our difficulties. I tried the "unofficial" hotels, but Prague was busy. Everywhere was full. It was only at the last gasp, and with anxiety increasing, that I found one sympathetic receptionist who was willing to try to do something to help us. The room was spartan in the extreme, but it was at least "a roof over our heads".

Reflecting on that uncomfortable adventure at this Christmas season, I felt sympathy with Joseph in what was essentially the same situation in Bethlehem. The town was busy and accommodation unavailable. Though Mary was far advanced in pregnancy, there seems to have been indifference to her need. "There was no room" - even in the inn. It was an innkeeper, at least sympathetic enough to allow them use his stable, who gave them a roof over their heads.

It is worth reflecting on the two factors common to these stories — in different ways and for different reasons. They are busy-ness and indifference. Both can damage spiritual health.

Indifference represents an absence of focus and vision alongside a lack of conviction and commitment. "There is nothing so fatal to religion as indifference," comments Edmund Burke. In public and community affairs, indifference to political responsibility creates flabbiness and, more dangerously, cynicism. In personal attitudes it becomes lukewarmness, and that God is quoted as finding unacceptable. But the worst feature of indifference is its inability to remain as indifference. It always, if undealt with, develops into something worse. Sin is frequently the product of untreated indifference.

Busy-ness too requires attention. Over-activity, though usually undertaken for what seem good reasons, can stifle spiritual growth. Prayer, for example, is probably limited to late-night spare moments, when physical and mental exhaustion reduce it to a gesture rather than a discipline.

The danger of over-busy-ness is its inherent capacity to eliminate the solitude so necessary to the spiritual life. It has to be questioned too for other reasons. It can be a rationalisation of our unwillingness to go to "the desert place". It may be a defence against the pain of life in general or a bereavement in particular. For the ability to be active, let us be profoundly grateful; blessed indeed are those who, like Martha, for our comfort are "care-full" and "troubled about many things". But there is also Mary's "better part", so commended by Jesus. That needs time and demands priority.

It is never a gain to replace *being* by *doing*. That is why Jesus struggled, not always successfully, to ensure his solitude.

Peace Restored

As we move into an unknown, uncertain and unpredictable new year, the gift that we all most need is that of inner serenity. And a gift it is, however meditation, relaxation and other human techniques may help to develop it. "My peace I *give* unto you," said Jesus to all his disciples. "Not as the world giveth, give I to you." The divine gift is, in essence, quite different from anything the world can offer. "Be still and know that I am God" exhorts the Psalmist, again. In a world of insecurity, literal and spiritual, having a still centre in the depths of our being remains the strongest element in our effort to cope with the strains and stresses, personal and corporate, that will surely face us in the coming year.

To many, this opening statement will feel to be no more than religious verbiage, irrelevant to the facts of life today. How can we possibly feel any sense of inner harmony and calmness faced as we are by the appalling cruelty of violent crimes, the scenes of starvation it is almost impossible to watch, the suffering of the innocent in serial killings, sectarian violence and sexual abuse? How can we now believe that there is a Providence "working his purpose out as year succeeds to year"? What purpose is there in prayer when pressing petitions for peace, healing and unity seem to remain unanswered? It is not surprising that, in a world like ours, religion is being dismissed as irrelevant, and faith is treated with indifference.

Yet the miracle persists! The Bible, though despised and rejected, attacked and abused, subjected to radical and often hostile criticism, survives and continues to be the highest-selling book in the world. The church, especially where it has been persecuted and faced with obliteration, is alive and strengthened by its sufferings. Many people testify to miracles of healing, reconciliation and inner change.

For those who have lost faith, hope and, especially, serenity, the Old Testament provides an encouraging reminder: "He heard my cry — *and gave me back my peace*".* The miracle of grace is expressed in words of restoration — reconciliation, reformation, regeneration, redemption, renewal. They all speak of the possibility of a return to a right relationship with God, and consequent loving relationships with others, self and earth. Peace is restored.

In a world which Jesus assured us would be one of tribulation, serenity can be recovered. The gift of God's peace is always on offer.

* Psalm 55, verse 18 (*New English Bible*)

PART V

THE HEALING
MINISTRY

The Healing Ministry

There has been a remarkable recovery of the healing ministry in virtually all the mainstream churches in the last twenty years. Those who sought a service of blessing by the laying on of hands used to have to search assiduously to find such a ministry, but now "Healing Services" are held in a great number of churches of many kinds. The restoration of the ministry of healing to a prominent place in contemporary worship is one of the significant signs of the times.

The word "recovery" is important. Such a ministry dare not be used as a gimmick that might attract more people into church. It is simply that the recovery of what the late Cameron Peddie called "the forgotten talent"* is now seen by so many to be a move "back to basics". When Jesus commissioned his disciples, he told them to "preach the gospel" and "heal the sick". The instructions appear to be of equal importance. The ministry of healing is not, therefore, just the province of eccentrics or extremists. It is a normal and crucial part of the church's life.

The disciples clearly understood Jesus's message about the connection between preaching and healing. Forbidden by the authorities to continue to preach in the name of Jesus, they asked for God's help in proclaiming the Gospel, namely that He would "stretch out His hand to heal", and that signs and wonders would authenticate the preaching of the Word.

It is important to do everything to ensure that the ministry of healing is carried out responsibly and in a spirit of humility (for arrogance and healing ministry simply do not go together). Three spiritual principles should always be applied where ministry is undertaken. They are

(i)   it must be encompassed in prayer

(ii) it must be founded on, and grounded in, the Word of God

(iii) it must be the subject of constant reflection under
the guidance of the Holy Spirit

The ambience of prayer is crucially important. Those who minister by laying on of hands are not the sources of healing. Christ is the healer and his ministering servants (whether they be individuals or, as was emphasised in healing services in Iona Abbey, the whole congregation) are but channels of grace. For that reason corporate prayer is of the utmost importance when the ministry is being offered "in Jesus's name".

While a distinction between the aim of the healing ministry (that is the wholeness of each seeker) and physical cure needs to be maintained, it is important to remember that Jesus interpreted his miracles of physical healing too as "signs of the presence of the Kingdom". While the purpose of the ministry of healing is to make people whole in soul, mind and spirit, that wholeness includes too the blessing of the body. Jesus did restore sight and hearing. He dealt with epilepsy. The dumb spoke and the lame walked. When John the Baptist (as I mentioned in an earlier Meditation**) seemed to question the authenticity of Jesus's Messianic role , he was directed to those very miracles as evidence of his claims. It is therefore right and proper that while those in need should be pointed towards wholeness of being as the desirable aim, they should feel wholly free to ask for physical healing. Many asked Jesus in his lifetime for that blessing, and they were granted their prayer.

* *The Forgotten Talent* by Cameron Peddie, published by Arthur James

** See *Go Forward!*, Number 57

The Spectrum of Healing

When Paul said that there were "diversities of gifts" but that they all had their source in that "selfsame Spirit", he laid down a spiritual principle of great importance. It puts paid to the kind of intolerance that claims "my ways", and only "my ways" accord with the will of God. There is an infinite variety in the way God deals with people and there are infinite manifestations of His presence in the gifts that people demonstrate. Sadly the arrogance that claims that a different way of doing things can only be detrimental, deluding and destructive, sets boundaries around that free-roving Spirit of God (like the wind, said Jesus, blowing where it chooses).

It is that sense of the many-splendour'd ways in which God works that enables us to appreciate the variety and wonder of God's gifts in healing. I see them as a spectrum of healing, incorporating both His gifts of creation and of redemption.

Let us reflect on the varied gifts offered for our healing. Sometimes one or more disciplines will meet the need. At other times, a different discipline will become the chosen resource.

(i) "Honour the doctor for his services", we read in Ecclesiasticus. "The doctor's knowledge gives him high standing and wins him the admiration of the great ... His skill comes from the Most High ..." (see chapter 38, verses 1-15).

No responsible ministry of healing denies or diminishes the place of medicine among God's gifts of creation. All who seek pastoral advice and help will not only be encouraged to see their GP, but exhorted to do so. Co-operation between medicine and religion is a primary concern in the field of healing ministry, and that co-operation is constantly growing. The truth is clear and simple: doctors, surgeons, nurses and all involved with them in medical and associated disciplines are part of the spectrum of healing.

(ii) Turn to the fields of psychiatry, psychotherapy, counselling and other varieties of therapeutic relationship and the same principle applies. Ministry to mental and emotional needs can be found in these disciplines. They too are in the spectrum of healing.

(iii) God uses people to minister to people. Through personal relations, whether it is informally as friends, more formally in pastoral care, or professionally through pastoral counselling and other forms of therapeutic relationships, people can be helped not only to feel better but to be better.

(iv) Music is another of God's gifts for our healing. For those unable to cope with verbal methods of help, music therapy can have a very important part to play.

(v) There are also valuable resources available in complementary medicines. That is a field which is much too wide, with unhelpful and unacceptable approaches within it, but there are, for example, "natural healing" methods within the field that are undoubtedly God's gifts of creation.

(vi) Supremely there is the church's contribution, the gifts of redemption, without which wholeness cannot be complete. Grace is conveyed through prayer, intercession, laying on of hands and, in some traditions, anointing. It is also the church's role to minister to the healing of the memories.

What a glorious spectrum of healing gifts, given in grace by the God whom we meet in variety and diversity rather than in exclusiveness and limitation!

The Healing of the Memories

O wad some Power the giftie gie us
To see oursels as ithers see us

It was Robert Burns, in his poem *To a Louse*, who penned this important sentiment. There are things that others know about us of which we ourselves are not aware. We should pay heed both to what they see in us and the way in which we present ourselves, and learn from it. We do not need to accept their impressions without question but we should, at least, carefully consider this new knowledge of ourselves.

Robert Burns's reminder that there is knowledge others have of us which we do not have, recalls other aspects of our self-knowledge. There is, for example, that knowledge we have have of ourselves which others share, a superficial knowledge but real. There is that darker area of our being of which *we* are aware, but of which, happily, others are not. Beyond that there is a further area of knowledge of which others do not have cognisance and of which we ourselves are unaware. It contains our hidden, unconscious memories. And some of these may well be unhealed.

This record of early experiences and the feelings associated with them (known in analytical psychology as "the unconscious") very much determines our behaviour, attitudes and the quality of our relationships in later life. If we had happy early experiences in those years which we cannot consciously remember, it is the more likely we will be secure as we grow older. If, however, our earliest feelings (again beyond the reach of our conscious memory) were unhappy — associated with rejection, absence of love, etc — it does not bode well for our ability to relate well, later on. It is part of the healing ministry to try to heal those hidden memories.

"Deep speaks to deep" says the Psalmist. Was he perhaps

suggesting that the depth of the divine love can reach right down to the ultimate depths of human need? The image of Jesus's descent into hell perhaps sheds light on the divine intention. There is no level of need that the grace which is "sufficient for all our needs" cannot reach.

There are various healing ministries directed toward the healing of the memories. First there is the patient, long-term approach of orthodox therapeutic relationship expressed in counselling, psychotherapy or analysis. Through a process of inter-action between the therapist and the person in need, memories may be brought into consciousness, faced and healed. Others, in a different tradition, will perhaps suggest (and use) some form of prayer counselling to attack the negative and, as they are believed to be, evil memories, and bring about inner reconciliation and peace. A third method, particularly practised by Esmond Jefferies at his Pin Mill healing centre,* is that of hypnosis within a prayerful context. As in psychotherapy, the approach is gentle, but the reaching of the hidden memories is much quicker. With the defences of the conscious mind removed, the hurtful, hidden memories are uncovered and released within an ambience of prayer and love.

To know oneself is an important aim. To attempt the fulfilment of that aim will be by the way this is felt to be safe and secure. However the healing of the memories is to be accomplished, it will be a process of pain and the suffering that ultimately contributes to our peace, ensuring that we can "Be still and know...".

It is a risky road and an adventurous one. That is why it all needs to happen within the grace of the Lord Jesus Christ and the community of love. But the ultimate blessing is real. Know yourself!

---

* The Pin Mill Fellowship, Albert Cottage, Pin Mill, Ipswich, Suffolk, England. The story of Esmond Jefferies' healing work is told in *The Power and The Glory* (Arthur James, 1991)

DENIS DUNCAN

a minister of The Church of Scotland, was formerly
Editor of *British Weekly* and Director of The Churches'
Council for Health and Healing. He was also Associate
Director and Training Supervisor at Westminster Pastoral
Foundation, Director of Highgate Counselling Centre and
of Hampstead Counselling Service, all in London.

Earlier he served in St Margaret's Parish
in Juniper Green, Edinburgh,
and Trinity-Duke Street Parish, Glasgow.

The focus of his current ministry is
"Proclamation through preaching, print and publishing".

He is Managing Director of Arthur James Limited.

The picture on the front cover, a view of the Sma' Glen near Crieff
in Perthshire, is used by permission of *The Perthshire Tourist Board*

A number of the symbol illustrations come, with permission, from
Saints, Signs and Symbols by W Ellwood Post, published by SPCK